A BLINDING DUTY

To Tony

Stewart Harris

A Blinding Duty

~

Stewart Harris

Pentland Books
Edinburgh · Cambridge · Durham

© Stewart Harris 2001

First published in 2001 by
Pentland Books
1 Hutton Close
South Church
Bishop Auckland
Durham

All rights reserved.
Unauthorised duplication
contravenes existing laws.

British Library Cataloguing in Publication Data.
A catalogue record for this book is available
from the British Library.

ISBN 1 85821 921 3

Typeset by George Wishart & Associates, Whitley Bay.
Printed and bound by Antony Rowe Ltd., Chippenham.

To Mary
without whose help
this book would never
have seen the light of day.

Contents

Acknowledgements

This book is dedicated to my wife Mary but more is called for. She went through the typescript many times wielding an editorial strength from which it benefitted enormously. My special thanks are due to her with an accompaniment of loving admiration.

In my early years, how could I have imagined the quality of life with her and its fulfilment with our children? I owe the latter, Catherine, Rosalind and Stephen and their families, a profound debt of gratitude for their constancy and love.

I am happy also to record the participation of my niece Gillian and her husband George Wilson of G and G Graphics in the preparation of this book. The application of their skills and warm-heartedness was most welcome and timely.

I acknowledge my great debt to my English teacher, the late Miss Dorothy Dean MA of Limpsfield in Surrey. She always made the subject sound so attractively precise and enjoyable.

I also acknowledge with the warmest of thanks the contribution made to my life by St Dunstans, the charity for the war-blinded disabled. I emphasise the part played by the Staff of the organisation whose devotion makes St Dunstans what it is and always will be.

My warm thanks also go to Max Hastings, Editor of the *London Evening Standard*. His generous and unstinting comments about my book are greatly appreciated.

Finally I record the debt I owe to my fellow wartime crew members whose friendship has been self-sustaining throughout sixty years. They are our wartime Captain Colin and his wife Peggy Taylor, Roy and Dorothy Evans, Cecil and Betty Anderson of Barrhead, Alberta, Billy and Margery Henderson, the late Douglas Inggs and his widow Margaret and Ronnie Chisholm of Seattle, US, whose life ended tragically so soon after the end of World War II. I pay tribute to them all.

Introduction

It is your duty to attempt to escape.
(Official briefing)

I am a member of, to my mind, a great family – my own. My marriage to Mary continues to have a special loving quality; our well-knit family life and the record of my own part in it may, perhaps, throw light on the pressing need to go forward that has always been within me.

Hopefully this book will provide the reader with an account of what happened to one of a generation totally affected and influenced by World War 2, who came from nowhere yet made a mark of a kind. However, I do not want you, my reader, to think this is a 'war' book. Indeed, it is not. In general those of us who were fortunate enough to survive the conflict do not wish to dwell excessively on the past.

My story may, perhaps, be read as a tiny piece of social history. It was formed during a period of profound change when young men and women grew up and went to war. They looked at life very differently and, in general, found their respect was heightened and extended to all classes of society, but they were people for whom deference to any of them did not sit comfortably.

After having been held as a prisoner-of-war I returned home in late February 1945 having been included in an exchange of sick and wounded prisoners through Switzerland. At that time I was not a very fit individual and needed much medical attention.

On my arrival I met our first child Catherine, then aged 15 months, and getting to know each other lasted a little while. Her acceptance of me into the family came in an off-beat way one day, when on the upper deck of a Brighton bus she announced to all the passengers: '*My Daddy's a German. He was locked up by the RAF!*'

Stewart Harris
November 1999
Hampshire

Foreword

I met Stewart Harris almost twenty-five years ago, when as an author researching a book on the wartime bomber offensive, I went to talk to him about his experiences as a Lancaster navigator. Almost everyone who took part in the Second World War endured experiences and trials beyond anything my own generation – I was born in 1945 – has known. Through my years researching books on the war, I have met many remarkable men who did extraordinary things when they were very young. Today, when I find myself interviewing job-seekers in their mid-twenties, I am often struck by how young and innocent they seem, alongside the men and women of Stewart's age group, who underwent so much before reaching the age at which a modern generation leaves university.

Stewart was a Surrey village boy, born in 1922 the son of a small shopkeeper and postmaster. He writes charmingly about his boyhood in a rural community only a short distance as the crow flies from London, yet it might have been a million miles for all he and his friends knew of the capital in the 1930s. He himself joined the Post Office as a teenager, then in 1939 volunteered for RAF aircrew. It is hard to overstate, more than sixty years later, how great was the romance of flight and of the RAF for those young men – and the sense of duty and patriotism which they displayed. Stewart's personal commitment was reinforced by the experience of craning his neck to watch the exploits of the Few above his own head, in Surrey in the summer of 1940.

He sailed to South Africa for training, was commissioned and sent home to Britain for operational training in 1942, where he married his sweetheart Mary. He began his operational flying career over Germany in one of the least effective and most dangerous RAF bombers of the wars, the Avro Manchester, in the famous 50 Squadron. Luckily for himself and his crew, they survived his early Manchester operations, and graduated to serve in the famous Lancaster, the best heavy bomber of the war. It was in a Lancaster of 619 Squadron in mid-1943 that they were attacked and badly damaged by a Luftwaffe night-fighter, then forced to bale out over Belgium.

Stewart became for a few days an evader, helped by brave Belgian civilians and *resistants* to join the long escape line across Europe to the Pyrenees. But one day while in hiding in Brussels, his hiding-place was betrayed. Captured by the Germans at gunpoint as he hid in a cupboard, he faced weeks of terrifying captivity in the hands of the Gestapo. The beatings, privations and hunger which he suffered permanently undermined his health. The husband of the couple who had sheltered him was later murdered in a concentration camp. Stewart thought himself fortunate indeed to be transferred as a prisoner-of-war to Stalag Luft III, the camp in one compound of which the legendary Great Escape and Wooden Horse sagas took place.

Stewart writes fascinatingly and movingly about everything that happened to him, first as a member of an RAF bomber crew – those very brave men who always knew that the odds were loaded against their own survival – and then as an evader and prisoner-of-war. He describes matter-of-factly terrible experiences, and sustains no illusions about some of those men whose behaviour was less than heroic or comradely. Early in 1945, he was repatriated to England, since even the Germans were obliged to concede that his failing health made him unfit for further operational service.

Perhaps the most bitter blow of all, however, befell him after his return home. He had just been granted a permanent commission in the Royal Air Force when a medical examination revealed that his sight had been permanently damaged by his experiences. He was told, horrifyingly, that he should expect to become blind within ten years. He left the RAF, and set out to make a new life in South Africa. Although he soon returned, he found his way into the oil industry, in which amid all manner of vicissitudes he remained for many years. His sight declined progressively, until by the end of the 1960s it was effectively gone. But he never allowed blindness to hamper his career or his enthusiasm for life, which persists to this day. Those of us who have led far less challenging lives can only bow with admiration to a man such as Stewart, who has done so much and endured so much with magnificent courage and determination. His story, which he tells so well, should be an inspiration to us all.

Max Hastings
May 2001

CHAPTER 1

Beginnings

The medical examination for my post-war commission seemed to be going well – no flat feet, no colour-blindness, no physical deformities – then came the bombshell!

'You will be blind in ten years time.'

In the light of my life so far how could I handle loss of vision and lead a life which did not keep Mary and the rest of the world in view? How many unexpected and potentially hazardous paths would have to be trodden? For a young man of twenty-four years this was indeed a daunting prospect. However, life goes on . . .

There is a small late-Victorian terraced residential quarter in Andover. The road names have royal connections: Alexandra, Osborne, Windsor and Balmoral can be found there. Until quite recently the area was known as The Park and was reached from the town by way of a rail-crossing and Junction Road. A branch line ran from Andover Junction (on the London-Salisbury-Exeter mainline) to Andover Town Station at the crossing.

I was born at 29 Balmoral Road on 27 March 1922 and my father, William (Bill) James Harris, had taken a lease on the house when he married in 1921 – about three years after he left the World War 1 Army. Dad's family had come from Exeter and he had grown up in the railway station house at Bulford Camp in Wiltshire, where my grandfather, Edwin (Ned) Harris was stationmaster. The site, which is marked today on a housing estate by a semaphore-type railway signal, was a busy one. A large proportion, if not all, of the forage fed to Army horses and used in army stabling on Salisbury Plain was received into and collected from the station. The stationmaster's pay, in those days, was supplemented by commission payments on the tonnage which went through his goods yard. Accordingly, Ned Harris was not badly off and, no doubt, was able to bring up his family in reasonable comfort for those days. He could afford the ale of which he was quite fond and he sent his children to good schools in Salisbury by train – as privileged passengers.

I have a fair memory of a tall man in a dark suit complete with waistcoat and watch-chain. Bulford Camp, like all stations of the day, had a Nestlé chocolate bar machine and on each of my visits to grandparents he would hide a bar in one of his waistcoat pockets. I remember the sight of a substantial watch-chain across his corpulence as clearly as I have always remembered the sound of a milk-churn being dragged across the station platform. Indeed, many unpleasant sounds today I automatically liken to the sound of the churn!

Aunt Dorothy, my father's younger sister, felt strongly about her father's income to the end of her days, for she was sure that it could have been better spent, in one way at least, by the fulfilment of her wish to go to teacher's training college at Bath. But this was not to be and a gentle grudge remained with a very likeable lady for many years.

There can be little doubt that my father's exposure to hay and straw at Bulford helped to make up his mind about his work after the end of the war. He joined an Andover forage firm, King Brothers, in or very near Andover Town Station – now long replaced by a Safeway store and car-park but with the Station Hotel still in evidence and the level-crossing a thing of the distant past. Dad's transport at work during those years after the war was a belt-driven Douglas motor-cycle and sidecar and a Riley 10 motor-car. The Douglas motor-cycle is remembered from their boyhood by my senior Andoverian friends; this contraption was frequently to be found standing outside King Brothers establishment.

Bill Harris never went outside England during his war service. It is almost certain that he was diagnosed as a cardiac risk and had a low medical category accordingly. He joined the Worcestershire Regiment which formed part of the Home Defence Force. During this period he met his friend, Cyril John (Jack) Gadd, a Bath man, Brasenose scholar and later, Keeper of the Assyrian Department at the British Museum. It seems probable that both men were medically unfit for combat duties. Their friendship ended with my father's death in 1966. They seemed to me to be an odd couple: the scholar and the railwayman's son. But there was a mutual, deep and complementary need. The one erudite, scholarly and an archaeologist, the other unambitious, a shopkeeper, in difficulty when expressing personal feelings, yet kindly, patient, an avid reader and a self-taught accountant.

In Bulford Church on Salisbury Plain there is a memorial list of those men from the parish who served in World War 1. My father's name is there just above a Major-General and I can imagine what my father, shown as a Lance-Corporal, might say: *'Quite the nearest I have ever been to a Field Officer!'*

My mother was of quite different stock and background. She was born Grace Mary Stewart in Bermondsey in South East London. Her father, Ernest, was an overseer at the South Eastern District Office of the London GPO. Her mother, Annie Emma, had a sister (Aunt Lizzie) whose husband, Tom Thomas, an East London property owner, gave financial help to my father from time to time. Additionally, Lizzie provided illusory background for the Thomas family by claiming that she had traced the family back to Count Jean-Marie Turgot, the minister and agro-economist to Louis XV and XVI of France! Perhaps someone from a later generation will, one day, go to work on this genealogically.

My mother was handicapped for most of her life by severe deafness, a difficulty which tested her own and my father's patience. Despite this affliction she was a very good pianist. In their later years this gentleness of my father was unfailingly bestowed upon her. However, my mother felt the weight of her handicap and was inclined to make it clear to everyone, in spite of their sympathy, that nothing ever went quite right for her.

So 29 Balmoral Road in Andover was the beginning for me. My father's work continued until around the end of 1924 when he lost his job with King Brothers, the forage merchants. The growth of the volume of internal combustion engined vehicles was liquidating horse transport and the forage business. My father used to talk about this period and, when I was much older, told me that he had once read a book about economic forecasting in the late nineteenth century; this volume opined that the roadway over London Bridge would be two feet deep in horse manure by 1900. Quite a shattering forecast!

Money must have been in very short supply for my parents. They moved out of the house and took rooms over Handley's the Chemist shop in the High Street and a little later quit Andover in mid-1925. Money help had been obtained from Uncle Tom Thomas who made available some £700 for my father to buy the lease of a small draper's business and sub-post office in Elm Park, Brixton. Its location was 150 yards from Brixton Hill and not far from my widowed maternal grandmother, Annie Emma, at Herne Hill.

I was to return to live in Andover again, sixty years later, and oddly, when I returned I was asked by the *Andover Advertiser* if they could print a feature on my life and adventures. I agreed, subject to there being printed an appeal for a lady called Ida, who, when twelve years old, had been a nursemaid-cum-pram pusher for me. The article was answered by Mrs Ida Wells within twenty-four hours of the issue of the newspaper – she was well into her seventies. People really do read local newspapers!

We lived in Elm Park, 'over the shop' in a three storey, narrow-fronted house. It was in a compact community which had changed little when I visited it some twenty-five years later. It runs eastward off Brixton Hill, almost opposite Brixton Prison. It was a street of poor quality Victorian terraced homes. We were to remain here for just four years and it is likely that our early removal was brought about by the termination of the lease and the revelation that the business was not viable.

Our house was in the centre of a row of other three-storey buildings where sawdust, cabbage leaves and general rubbish littered the gutters and pavements. Butcher, baker, dairyman, newsagent, greengrocer and bootmender were there. Clements the butcher cut himself regularly and seriously. Mr and Mrs Webb, the greengrocers, quarrelled loudly and threw vegetables and fruit at each other in full public view. Johnson the grocer, next to us, had an off-licence section where he thrashed his profits each weekend by over-indulgence. He loved his gramophone and in summer would have a drunken sleep at his upper back window, while the records could be heard overrunning on the turntable. Fortunately for us on one occasion, he was able, at a wakeful and sober moment, to shout an alarm when intruders climbed the corrugated iron fence at the rear of our premises, attracted, no doubt, by the prospect of their seizure of funds and negotiables in the sub-post office. It was an attempt to break in that was foiled.

I recall the post office counter set up on a low stage at the end of the shop. There were frequent shopping calls by Brixton prison officers, some of whom would buy chocolate for prisoners.

The greengrocer's van, which always stood in the road, was a commercial manifestation of the Ford Model T and the sound of its gear-box is still clear to me. I recall the ox-drawn covered wagon of the Atora Suet Company which delivered to the grocer; another memory is of deliveries made to the off-licence and the foetid smell and splashing sound of the brewer's dray horses relieving themselves precisely outside the shop where we lived. Truly a salubrious neighbourhood!

We watched the annual Veteran Car Run to Brighton and on one such occasion Uncle Tom Thomas caused a stir by dropping his walking stick into the central cable channel which helped the trams to climb Brixton Hill.

In those days the buses still had solid tyres and their drivers sat out front exposed to all weathers. Outside Lambeth Town Hall on Armistice Day on 11 November 1927 and 1928, I stood in a scene of total stillness for two minutes with my father as all drivers left their seats to stand in the road; hats were removed and everyone was absolutely silent.

I was taken by my father to the cinema next to Lambeth Town Hall, to see my first film, 'The Battle of the Falkland Islands' (not to be confused with the later war in Margaret Thatcher's time) – I was taken home in a state of terror!

My brother, Robert William, was born at home on 7 January 1926 and at about that time I went down with a serious bout of double-pneumonia after a series of childhood illnesses. Two treatments of those events remain in my memory: the chest poultices (which one could roll up into small missiles) and having brandy applied to my lips at a critical juncture.

When I was well again I found a family of three in possession of the third floor of our home, the father being Detective-Constable Robert Fabian, and Scotland Yard records describe him as follows:

Detective Superintendent Robert Fabian was *Fabian of the Yard* to the millions who followed the films and television series inspired by his exploits. He joined the Metropolitan Police in 1921 and spent most of his career in London's West End, especially in the seamy Soho district. By the time he won the King's Police Medal for bravery in 1939 for disarming an IRA bomb found near Piccadilly Circus, Fabian had gained a reputation as a fearless crime investigator who knew the haunts of criminals and their methods. He headed the famous Flying Squad from

December 1944 until 1947 when he took over as chief of the Murder Squad, a post he was to hold until his retirement two years later.

My memory is of a man who wore a powerful eau-de-toilette and who fell off a roadside kerb in Brixton and broke his ankle; Mrs Fabian cried a lot when he came home on that occasion.

My father and mother were not great communicators. Perhaps it was their view that a generation gap was a gap to be observed. It was many years before they considered it reasonable to tell the children anything. Accordingly, quite suddenly, we moved in to live with my grandmother Annie at Herne Hill in early 1929 and I was sent to school for a term at the LCC Dulwich Hamlet infant school. My father then disappeared for some time; he certainly did not stay with us. Maybe it was a mother-in-law problem because I later learned that Grandma Annie was a sharp-tongued lady. Whatever the problem, and wherever he lived, it is clear that he looked for another business to buy – with Tom Thomas's loan money. He succeeded in the little village of Tatsfield, on the borders of Surrey and Kent.

So, at the last gasp of 1929, immediately after Christmas, aged seven years plus, I arrived at the shop, house and home. It was to play quite a part in forming my attitudes in the life ahead. I recall strongly my feeling of curiosity when first we arrived and I scampered round the premises to have my first look at the place. I somehow knew then that I had become an island, an individual. Nothing had been said to me about a removal from Grandma Annie Stewart's house and Tatsfield came out of the blue; I was suddenly in a different world. London had disappeared without trace. It could be argued that I did not remember what my parents might have said but in retrospect I had a strong sense of abruptness. Maybe the end of the first seven year phase of my life had begun to take effect and my psyche had begun to stir.

The people from whom the business had been bought, Mr and Mrs Firrell, had elected to stay on in order that a better takeover might be achieved and all our goods and chattels were crowded into the largest bedroom. I had never seen my mother and father in bed together and they took good care that, in these cramped quarters, my brother, aged three years, and I should not have our knowledge extended and we were put safely behind a screen! Years later my own family did not experience that sort of shelter from worldliness and reality.

CHAPTER 2

Village Life

Village life quickly proved to be hard and basic. It went on being so until I left it finally to join the Royal Air Force in 1941. My parents and my brother remained there, the latter until 1943 when he joined the Royal Navy and the former completed thirty years to 1959 when the business was sold. My children and grandchildren would find the level of quality of our life at Tatsfield quite unbelievable, unacceptable and so far down the social ladder that one questioned the existence of a ladder. Our situation was clear. We were at a very low ebb and would remain so for several years to come. But I never knew how my father felt about it. It did not seem to arise as an issue at any time. Such was not the case with my mother.

The village is in Surrey, placed in a curious blip in the county boundary with Kent. If one views the North Downs from the south the village lies at about 700 feet a mile northward from the top of the escarpment. Further north, across a valley and atop Polesteeple Hill, lies Biggin Hill. Four miles to the south-east is Westerham, a couple of miles into Kent. Tatsfield was in a near cul-de-sac, having one approach from the Croydon-Westerham road and two narrow lane exits which came to a single crossing of the Kent border at Biggin Hill. It was delightful in summer months but viciously cold in winter, catching the bad weather from any direction and snow in remarkable depth. The high point of the Downs was precisely at the turn-off to Tatsfield from the Croydon-Westerham road. Close to that junction, in 1929 and for several years thereafter, there stood a large lighthouse acting as a guide to incoming and outgoing passenger aircraft from Paris and Croydon. Three hundred yards, just north of west from the lighthouse, across a field, lay the BBC monitoring station and a mile down the Tatsfield road one walked into the village. The first buildings were seen just beyond the pond on the Green. They consisted of a block of three shops, the third of which was my father's; two further buildings, quite close, were the bakery and the Old Ship public-house. All these made up the centre of the village.

7

The Harris shop was a general store and post office, sharing the frontage of the Parade with a coal merchant/greengrocer and the Tatsfield Working Men's Club. The three establishments boasted a shaky verandah under which shoppers loitered or took shelter.

The village main street ran down the side of our end of the building where the butcher, newsagent, draper and a grocer-competitor could be found within fifty yards.

Immediately behind the shop was a living-room which looked out on the bakery and the pub. Behind this room one came to the kitchen and thence to the store, an all-purpose warehouse of lean-to brickwork construction with corrugated-iron roofing.

There was no electricity, no gas or main drainage and no bus service. The population, in the widespread parish, was 650 persons. A tiny minority, the well-off, had motor cars; the rest walked to catch the 403 Sevenoaks bus to Croydon or Westerham a mile away on the main road and close to the airways lighthouse. A lucky few had bicycles.

One advantage we had in later years was the acquisition of a quarter-acre plot of land nearby which my father developed from pasture-land into a very attractive and well-planned garden. Before he bought the plot he used the area, under licence, as a bonfire site. Every few days he would carry a sackful of rubbish across the green, empty it and burn the contents. It burned well for it contained grease-proof wrapping paper which had covered 56 pound blocks of butter and margarine, hambones stripped of their meat, bones taken from sides of bacon, sweepings from the shop-floor, empty boxes etc., etc. A GPO parcel sack would easily contain a week's collection and would await my father's attention in the store.

The store was used as a letter mail sorting area and a place for the collection of parcels for carriage to the main sorting-office at the Sevenoaks GPO. Unfortunately, one day the postman-driver took away the outward parcel post plus another of His Majesty's parcel sacks filled with a choice selection of rubbish. All the sacks were emptied onto the Post Office parquet flooring at Sevenoaks!

Some time later my father received a 'phone call as follows:

'Mr Harris,' said the Superintendent, 'You are one of our most reliable sub-postmasters but we really cannot allow you to use the GPO bags in the service of your other business, especially as we seem to have been drawn into that activity. I hope I make myself clear?'

Tatsfield could hardly have been more rural and despite some development it remains so today. The Church is atop the Downs with glorious views to the south and west – even to Chanctonbury. The nine hundred year-old building is a fifteen minute walk from the village centre but rather closer to the wealthier part of the parish. In those days the residents of note were Sir Henry Theobald, KC, the blind advocate, the Compton-Skinners, the Godards at the Old Rectory (C.W. Godard was the eponymous head of a company which held the Royal Appointment to HM Queen Mary as a supplier of ladies' handbags). Others were the Gorings of the Goring Hotel group, Henry Carr, RA, the Leweson-Gowers at Titsey Place and, a distance across the Kent boundary, the Churchills at Chartwell near Westerham. From time to time the film actor Charles Laughton and his wife Elsa Lanchester were resident. Years later came Harold Lotery, the wealthy military uniform manufacturer (one of the early acquisitions of the fated financier Jim Slater Group, Slater Walker), the Verney-Caves (later Earl Braye) and last and certainly least, a Mr and Mrs Donald Maclean of the Burgess and Maclean double-spy act. Their escape is immortalised on a cleverly designed plaque near the village pond.

When Mr Godard's daughter was married from the Old Rectory, I delivered the congratulatory telegrams. Later in life, Kenneth Godard, her brother, became one of my long-lasting friends. We had the same birthdate in March, although the year was different. He had been the local Scoutmaster and his widow, Monica, is still resident in the village at well over eighty years of age.

When I returned from Germany in 1945 Kenneth told me that when he heard I was missing in action his conscience pricked him so badly that he volunteered for overseas duty; he was fourteen or fifteen years older than I was. His application was granted and as a Staff Sergeant he was shipped to India. On arrival he was commissioned and soon reached the rank of Major – with 'the cushiest job' he had ever had! We both loved to talk and laugh about his military good luck and his fortunate and active conscience.

It was he who was in command when the Tatsfield troop of Boy Scouts built a rope bridge over a pond near to the Scout headquarters. I volunteered to attempt to walk across the bridge spanning water which cattle had stood in for generations. The construction collapsed and I came out covered from head to foot in what one might expect in such a place. We returned to the Scout hut where buckets of water were thrown over my naked body. I was taken home wrapped in the Union flag – surely an honourable return!

The shop dimensions were 25 feet by 12 feet and as one passed through the living-room and kitchen and, finally into the store, one was confronted by a heavy back door and then outside steps where one came to the yard, the stables and coal sheds. These steps were much used by postmen, millers, paraffin sellers and suppliers of all kinds of goods. Sundry callers used them either simply to reach the store or to ask whether, shop closing time being long past, my father would oblige them by supplying an emergency loaf or a little bacon perhaps? Many a pheasant, hare or brace of partridge could be found there in the late evening as tokens of appreciation for help to all types of village people – including professional poachers to whom Dad had sold gin-traps across the counter! Harry Roberts of that ilk claimed that he was able to creep up behind a hare whilst it sat in the middle of a field and fall on it – fair game on both sides I would say!

Callers had to be careful on Friday nights for the back-door might suddenly fly open and a long tin bath would be emptied in quick time down the steps! The village policeman had a narrow escape from a feet-soaking when he called one such evening to seek information, advice, or a favour. Mr Miles the farmer-milkman also called daily at the back door. A jug would be brought to him by my mother for a pint to be dispensed by a measure from a lidded milk pail. Mr Miles had a long nose and a short chin. In winter a crystal clear drop would hang from his nose placed almost vertically above the open pail! My mother suggested that Miles, almost certainly, had more milk left than he expected at the end of his day. She wished he would close the lid of his pail more rapidly. I was to meet his look-alike in Freetown harbour, Sierra Leone, at Christmas in 1941.

The winter winds swept north-south directly through the whole house. The flames in the three oil lamps in the shop and the lamp in the living room would leap and smoke with every draught and had immediately, so many times, to be adjusted. The kitchen had no lamps and was 'illuminated', when required, by candlelight. The same lighting conditions applied to the store. Here there were bins for all types of millings including maize, wheat, middlings and oats; it was by candlelight on the lids of these wooden bins that letter sorting would start at 6.15 am each working day morning. If one threw open these bins quickly one could slaughter six mice at a time with a metal scoop as a weapon!

Two postmen and one postwoman sorted the incoming mails from Sevenoaks – and in those days postmen still wore the shako as headgear, but they went out of use in the early thirties.

There was no heating save for a coal-burning kitchen range and a fire-place in the living room. The kitchen had a cold water tap only. (An electric water heater would not come for some years when the whole village was electrified.) The single lavatory was in the store in a modest sized cupboard just next to a hand-pump which dispensed paraffin. There were three bedrooms and no bathroom. Water for washing and for hot drinks had to be heated on the range or on a 'Beatrice' paraffin stove: it took half an hour per kettle boiling. We had two of these stoves and to provide water for bathing in the tin bath was a long job for a family of four. Needless to say, my brother and I shared the same water.

In winter the kitchen was desperately cold. The table was placed over a large trap-door to the cellar where one descended toward the surface of two feet of water. It did not pay to lose one's footing on the steps – my father forgot the water just once! We could thus boast an ice-room under the floor in summer. The gentle village idiot named Kruger (an index of his birthdate perhaps) would be hired in the warm weather to paddle in the cellar and empty it of water, bucketful by bucketful, throwing the contents through a small doorway which opened onto the public footpath down Westmore Road. Customers and/or other pedestrians who were unaware of this operation learned by trial and error but they did not mind; it was all part of the village scene!

I save the most intrusive problem to the last point of this description. The living room contained the switch-board for the Tatsfield telephone exchange and the kitchen accommodated the circuit boxes and fuses; the store had a bank of batteries which served the phone system. We were never quiet, never alone, always interrupted, day or night, at Christmas or at Easter or any other time. In a thunderstorm or in other exceptional atmospheric electrical conditions, a blue light played and spluttered over the fuses in the kitchen, sometimes alarmingly. It must have been the lowest-priced business my father could have found. Luckily, just after the outbreak of World War 2 in 1939, the telephone exchange was removed and the new equipment housed elsewhere in the village. It was one of the earliest automatic exchanges in the whole country. Not before time.

The shop's customers came from the village centre whilst another competitor grocer served the wealthier section, appropriately at the west-end of the village. I was to pass this shop four times daily on my way to and from the village primary school, a half-mile away from home. There were no school dinners so one came home for whatever was available. My father served on the board of management for some years but resigned in protest at the frequency of use of the cane by the headmaster. Motor traffic was negligible and parents were spared any anxiety for their children in those days.

My father pronounced that we would not be admitted to village life for fifteen years but this proved to be a wild over-estimate. As a child let loose in utterly rural surroundings, free to go in almost any direction through woods, fields, hills and valleys, young village friends were made quickly. Village parents had work as road-sweepers, on farms, at large houses, chalkpit quarries and local water works. London commuters motor-cycled to South Croydon but there were very few of these. Homes were small, their occupants' wages averaged 30 shillings (£1.50) weekly. One was quickly made welcome.

The lack of main drainage was clear for most privys were in the garden and some homes were individually distinguishable by their very own aroma, depending how close the loo was to the back door! We had a water-closet and cess-pool – now politely known as domestic drainage. If the cess-pool overflowed (it also served the two horses in the stables), the overflow was carried by a pipe into the gutter of Westmore Road, the village main street. No-one ever complained. When the contents were routinely emptied they were hand-pumped into a horse-drawn tank, which was then taken across the green in front of the shop to a field where it was quickly emptied. It was here that my father bought land to make his garden and to prepare for a new shop which was never built. It is not surprising that the plants, fruit-trees and vegetables flourished apace!

For three years from late 1929 it was village life pure and simple. I was a choirboy at the church, part-time errand boy for my father and his customers, companion to the coal-merchant on his cart and his coal trucks at Westerham station and in the stables at the back of the house and shop buildings. The horses, the coal dust, the stable manure-heap, the paraffin smell at the rear of our home, all combined in an enrichment of atmosphere which pervaded everywhere. I came home blackened from head to foot after coal-heaving from the rail coal-trucks and smelling like a paraffin rag when I carried two-gallon can deliveries to a customer. It was an early introduction to hard physical work. When not at school I also performed as post-office telegram messenger-boy. It was a far cry from the working conditions of my favourite author Anthony Trollope in his career in the Post Office.

For my duties I had one pair of trousers and one pair of boots and I can remember to this day the feel of my damp clothes as I dressed on cold winter mornings. Again, I am sure Trollope and Rowland Hill did not have such a tough series of duties in early life.

My father supplemented his income by becoming Secretary of the local Working Men's Club and eventually was much in demand from all the local organisations as an accountant and auditor.

I always thought his beginnings as Secretary of the Working Men's Club to be tactically flawed. As a committee member he advocated the halving of the secretary's fee and then promptly got the job himself! Despite his efforts, however, there were periods of shaky credit-worthiness and crises in the business from time to time. He could advise others how to keep their books but was singularly disorganised in his own affairs. And the telephone exchange continued to intrude both day and night. But whatever our true plight may have been we shared it with the rest of the village folk.

As time went by my father became known as 'The Guv'nor' and respect for him grew throughout the village. We became Tatsfield village people.

The village folk were close-knit and inter-related: the Higgs, Shrubbs, Smiths, Boltons, Lugtons, Burbages and Standings were the village backbone. Few could read or write but all knew if the wrong change had been given in the shop.

One Mrs Higgs would deal with your body when you died, whilst another of that name provided you with ill-gotten game! The Burbages were into most of the local economy whilst Shrubbs, Higgs and Smiths were all expert big-house gardeners or long-serving farm-workers – and poachers!

There was one rag and bone merchant, Bob Raymond, who built his own cart from cast-off wheels and thrown-away wood, the whole contraption being pulled by a small donkey. Bob could not afford to buy beer in the Old Ship but regularly purchased a packet of beer making material from my father for production at home.

Tom Dann, a six foot three giant, was a woodcutter and coppice man. He wore the same clothes, summer and winter, but made a concession on Sundays by removing his cap and sporting a battered trilby for his sabbath pint!

Tom Rushen, the second woodcutter, had worked so long at his job that his finger-tips bore no prints. Attempts were made by the police to take his fingerprints when the Working Men's Club was burgled (he being a committee man and aid to the steward) but they failed to get any prints. Tom stood behind me in the choir-stalls at church and sang only one or two notes. Curiously, it worked quite well but I would rather have stood behind him!

The village was electrified in 1933-34 – an exciting innovation and at the Tatsfield Horticultural Show in August 1935 we heard George V make his first national broadcast. In 1936 he was dead and the state funeral was to be broadcast on the wireless. My father thought we really should listen to the broadcast events and bought our first radio, an Ekco. This purchase brought another, long-lasting change: he became used to listening to the one o'clock lunch-time news and hit upon the idea of closing the shop for the lunch-hour. Thereafter and every day he would stand at the shop door as one o'clock approached and as soon as the first pip of the Greenwich Time Signal sounded, the door was slammed unceremoniously and vigorously.

Gossip and rumour were rampant but humour was far from absent. One lady who drew a pension at the post office and could write, penned a note to my father one day which ran:

'Dear Mr Harris, Please let my Rose have my pension this week. I am too busy upside down with the workmen.'

There was also:

'My Ruth is in hospital, Mr Harris, and she's very sick. They've started giving her gin!'

Father: 'Surely not, Mrs Higgs. I think you must mean oxygen.'

And another:

'Mr Harris, do you sell Epsom Salts?'

Father: 'Yes, in two ounce packets.'

'Right. Thank you. I'll take two packets and four toilet rolls please.'

Mrs Morley was a village lady and a great character – it was said that she had gypsy forebears. Shortly after we arrived in the village she was widowed in very unusual circumstances. Her husband had been a road-sweeper (lengthsman) who had long been accustomed to eating bread and cheese for his midday meal by the roadside. He always took an egg with him which he broke into a cup, applied salt and pepper and swallowed the lot in a single gulp. One day, in the preparation of this appetiser he failed to notice that the top of the salt or pepper dispenser had fallen into the broken egg. In taking his customary gulp he swallowed part of his cruet. Whether it went down his wind-pipe or his oesophagus I do not know, but I do know he died as a result of his haste to take lunch.

The present National Health Service would have dealt with the situation I am certain, but there was no way in which the medical profession could have responded to the plight of a road-sweeper in those days.

Mrs Morley had taken his death bravely but as the years went by, in my certain knowledge, she became unsteady on her feet, a condition not entirely brought on by increasing age. She carried about her an aroma that was, beyond reasonable doubt, not Chanel No. 5! She was outwardly a friendly old thing but rum at twopence or threepence a tot had taken her over!

Bert Lewis took Morley's road-sweeping job. He worked flat out but his progress along the roadside was dead slow. Jimmy Honey, an earlier holder of the job, cashed his quarterly Surrey County Council pension voucher over my father's counter in the sum of two shillings and sixpence (12.5p). With a weekly state pension of ten shillings (50p) he and his wife, a dear old lady, got by somehow.

The pattern of my life changed significantly from 1932-36. In April 1932 I was sent to Oxted County Secondary School three years after its opening and I was pupil number 148. The total number of girls and boys in my first year was 100 with 7 teachers. It now holds 1947 pupils and 115 teachers.

I had failed to obtain a county scholarship and cost my father £4 per term thereafter and it was difficult for him to find that amount of money; the shop turnover was pitifully low, averaging £30 to £40 per week at best, with a very narrow profit margin. The post office salary was low – but helpful.

The significant watershed for me was when I started at Oxted School, which I reached by cycling the four miles in every kind of weather. I was parted from my friends: Jim Streets (died of wounds in

Italy), Harold Mays, the policeman's son, Jim Standing (later Chief Inspector Metropolitan Police), Doug Street, Ron Streatfield (Conspicuous Gallantry Medal 1944) and Dion Lawrence (missing on RAF operations as an air-gunner).

The appearance of my red and black quartered school cap and blazer with school badge set me apart from these village boys and I could not convince them that I was still the same. The suspicion was that I was taught different things from them and that amongst these was an ability to practice ju-jitsu – a curious idea as I was never that aggressive anyway. In retrospect I have always remembered a strong feeling of disappointment at that time. I wanted the connections to go on but it was not possible. I was ten years old. When my village friends reached fourteen years of age they went out to work and I went on with my education. But I did qualify at that age for my first pair of long grey flannel trousers!

I did renew contact with some of my old friends after the war. The warmth of those reunions revealed a common understanding and rejection of the ingrained village social levels of the past. I was glad and have never flinched from the attitude that society as a whole should reflect appropriate levels of respect for one another. Deference is demeaning and not to be considered.

When I went to the County School I was clearly a village boy with little to say because there was nothing in me that had to be expressed. I had virtually no sense of the need to work at school and this state persisted for most of my time up to age fifteen and matriculation. I must have shown some leadership potential, however, for I was made school prefect, vice-captain of House and captain of 2nd XI cricket and fixture secretary for the school. My memory of it all was that it was too much trouble. My father made only two visits to the school. The first was to be told that I was a hopeless case for a matriculation success. The only hope for me was that I might become what was known in the trade as a slow-developer. The second visit, a year later and at the end of my schooling, Dad came to see me in a Clemence Dane play – and left proudly, I believe. I remember he gave me ten shillings for getting a good matriculation result – six credits. The 50 pence equivalent today would not please many school leavers, but I felt good.

There are memories which stand out. None has anything to do with school or achievement. Most touch on the emotions and continue to do so. They mark, perhaps, the development of deeper feeling and in hindsight, were the first signs of an awareness of the whole environment; the stirring of emotion and a growing feeling for living things.

My foremost memory of Tatsfield is what it taught me of the unspoiled countryside: the view over Titsey and way beyond, the spectacular sight of open country from the ridge overlooking the chalkpits and lime kilns above Oxted, the depth of Ship Woods and its primroses and the sight of cowslips hiding away off White Lane.

To me the impressive first sight of a large country house was profoundly revealing. It was the Leveson-Gower home called Titsey Place, seen from their private cricket ground where my father played in a village match between Tatsfield and the Titsey Estate. It was there that I first heard my father swear when he was out first ball and muttered:

'There's a hole in the bloody bat!'

A memory of the walk from the village to Tatsfield Church and the mild anxiety of being at the bottom of Church Hill and so close to the Pilgrim's Way on any November 5th, when local folklore had it that a lone horseman would be heard, at 5.30 in the afternoon, galloping through to warn other Gunpowder Plot conspirators at Westerham that the game was up.

There were two destructive fires to remember: the first, that of the village Manor House, seen across the valley from my bedroom window in the early morning hours, completely ablaze. The villagers were appalled at the loss and the incident was discussed at length for some time. What outlasted this talk was the memory of the exploits of 'Tatsfield Fire Brigade' which turned out to lend a hand.

The owner of the one petrol-pump village garage was a retired London County Council fireman. He had bought a second-hand fire-engine from Holmwood, a village near Dorking. This red monster, mounted on a Ford Model 'T' chassis, was taken over most of the time by chickens which perched on the running boards and brass rails. Retired fireman Tommy Watson, with his three sons, Sid, Frank and Dick (a baker by trade) leapt into action as soon as they heard that the Manor House was burning. Any recalcitrant chickens were chased away, the engine was started and away they went. All went well until they swept round the very sharp turning near the village school, 500 yards from the fire, when Dick, the baker, fell off. Father Watson was in full cry and would not stop. Fortunately, Dick (a mainstay of the Tatsfield football team) was the fittest of his sons and quickly caught up with the rest of the family at the scene. Dick (known as 'Dona' because he made the village doughnuts) was teased for a very long time.

In 1936 the only difference between the Tatsfield Fire Brigade and the Keystone Cops was that the former was a real life act!

The second fire was the glass Crystal Palace at Sydenham seen in absolute clarity at a distance of about twelve miles, burning like a beacon. The next day a friendly landmark was no more.

One other event on a cold and wet winter's evening affected every member of the village community. For me it began when I was coming home from school, climbing the steepest section of Titsey Hill as it mounted to the top of the North Downs. The beech trees overhead formed a black tunnel and there was a soft roar of the wind in the dense leafless branches. I was within half a mile of the airways lighthouse, so the sound of a low flying aircraft overhead en route to Croydon Airport, the London airport of the day, was not unusual. What did surprise me was the abrupt stop of the engine noise but I suppose I convinced myself that I was mistaken and nothing could possibly be wrong.

Within half an hour I was home to find that the shop, the house and the village was humming. My father was at the switchboard of the telephone exchange. An aircraft had flown into the ground a half mile north of the centre of the village and all aboard were killed in a Sabena Junkers Ju52 passenger aircraft.

Débris and the remains of the passengers were strewn about a wood in the centre of which was the lovely house and garden called 'Mosscroft' – the home of Mr and Mrs O'Reilly. Only a flint track led to this house, one of the near-inaccessible parts of Tatsfield. Very few villagers were able to reach the scene quickly and I remember how shaken the village policeman was as it fell to him to be among the first on the scene. He was profoundly disturbed and when retiring to bed the next night needed to have his bedroom light burning throughout the hours of darkness.

Within two hours the village was alive with scores of London taxi-cabs and pretty soon after journalists were knocking on our parlour window to seek the latest information from the telephone exchange operator – my father. I have always had a strong belief that money changed hands for up-to-the minute information. It was an appalling night, one to remember.

The next day the newspapers were a revelation. The gulf between the truth and the stories printed by the press was unbelievable. The only accurate facts given were the number of the dead and the identification of Sir Thomas Carden, the British tank design adviser and Government military consultant. This early impression of the heights of Press irresponsibility has remained with me all my life and has often been repeated on a variety of personal and national business occasions.

One more incident must be recorded. It happened one Saturday and for some years thereafter deeply affected my view of and attitude toward my father. Just before leaving home to play in a rugby match he asked me to buy a branded preparation which allegedly cleaned chimneys when burnt in fireplaces. This I was to do after rugby and I duly made the purchase with the sixpence given to me and secured a penny change. The packet, as far as I could see, bore no price, so I repaired to the local station to buy a bar of chocolate from a machine. I put the penny in the slot of the first one in the ticket office but made a bad selection and found myself with a brand-new platform ticket in my hand! My memory does not serve me well as to what my thoughts might have been at the moment of receipt of that ticket – intense disgust must have been one.

I returned home and my father duly set fire to the cleaner. The exercise went awry and he was seized with a furious spasm of coughing from which he was slow to recover. When he did his anger was directed at me; the price of the item was fivepence he said and where was his penny? I dishonestly claimed that the price was sixpence but I was shown the package upon which the true price was written. I was accused of the depths of deceit and dishonesty, I was disowned and threatened with a visit to the local policeman – only a hundred yards away. I never forgot the threat of the police – or forgave my father. I could not expunge the incident from my mind – and, as I was to find out years later, neither could he.

19

CHAPTER 3

The First Job

There was some discussion at home about my future – but not much. My school record was unspectacular but some enquiries were made and a prospectus received from the Wye Agricultural College; however, the upshot of this was that the training course was too expensive. My own preference at that time was to join the Royal Engineers. The daughter of the coal merchant, Dorothea Kent (on whose father's cart I had spent so much time at an earlier age) had married a Royal Engineer Sergeant and I saw no reason why I should not follow him into the army; he retired as a Lieutenant Colonel after the war. This idea was turned down flat by my parents and, in common with a feature of family life in those days, I found myself doing as I was told.

I applied for a position within the Civil Service as a Sorting Clerk and Telegraphist at the Crown Post Office at Caterham in Surrey. In September of 1938 I began training at the Central Telegraph Office at St Martins Le Grand in the City of London. 'Telegraphy' meant learning to type and to use a teleprinter; 'sorting' meant sorting and despatching mails from Caterham to other delivery centres and by Royal Mail travelling post offices throughout the UK. There was a further duty for which detailed training was necessary: I had to become proficient at selling the services of the GPO behind the post office counter and to learn how to account for it all at the end of the day.

I recall meeting Major Tryon, MP, the Postmaster-General of the day, at the counter school; he came into the instruction room in bright sunlight and I had an unbelievable view of the most gravy-bespattered waistcoat I had ever seen or was likely to see again!

I was despatched into lodgings not far from the Brigade of Guards Depot in Upper Caterham. My pay started at £1 8s. per week and the GPO certainly got its money's worth. The duty periods were varied, one starting at 4.17 am – a time of day quite foreign to me. It soon occurred to me that at sixteen years old I was doing the same work and accepting the same responsibility levels as those of colleagues three times my age – but it mattered little. The shop steward, a man who stood 6 feet 2 inches tall, was not a man to argue with when he suggested that I was joining the Union of Post Office Workers – was I not? He, Hawksworth, was a senior postman and an ex-Sergeant of the Grenadier Guards and the salt of the earth.

The Postmaster, Harry Campkin, was a good leader whom nobody seemed to like, but who obviously ran a tight office. At my age it took a time for me to get used to being called just 'Mister' – no Christian or surname.

There was one extremely efficient and effective lady who was outrageously lesbian; her partner worked at the Croydon Head Office. At that time I was clearly on an upward learning curve.

Perhaps the most sympathetic member of the whole office was an ex-Regimental Sergeant-Major of the Rifle Brigade named Father Charlton. He was one of two Head Postmen and although I did not fall within his authority, I jumped like everyone else when he exercised it. He lived near my lodgings and his brother-in-law was the well-known Guardsman Regimental Sergeant-Major Brittain. When they both boarded a bus together one could see how much the vehicle springs had to give way! I liked Father Charlton; he helped my streetwise quotient to take off. Bill Jordan was the other Head Postman and at that time was an elected member of the Caterham & Warlingham Urban District Council and later was to become its Chairman and a Justice of the Peace; he too was a gentleman and a retired senior ranked ex-serviceman.

The intricacies of the national postal sorting system were revealed to me – as was the lax security regime, discovered after the war by the criminal class and by me early in my short Post Office service. One of my new colleagues attempted to drop-kick a Lloyds Bank High Value Packet (HVP) into his caged desk. It burst, showering used banknotes everywhere. Panic-stricken restorations were made. We anticipated a big back-fire from almost any quarter but fortunately for us there was none.

In my experience of Post Office counter duties I came face to face with every kind of gentle, awkward, rude, eccentric and tiresome customer. The charming pianist Irene Scharrer (her recorded rendering of Litov's Scherzo was brilliant) and the friendly Sir Adrian Boult were regular customers. One delightful old lady wanted me to send a lace handkerchief to her daughter by telegram. I had gently to say that such things could not be done; she still gave me an apple pie for Christmas! There was also a younger and wealthier lady whose corsage was worn so low that the male members of staff on duty fought to give service as soon as she came through the swing-doors! There were some persistent would-be fraudsters to boot.

An important extra-curricular activity had begun: I had the good fortune to meet Mary and we were writing frequently to each other. She would come to stay with her aunt at Quarry Farm in Godstone and would sweep by the office in a car on a Sunday morning with her relatives on their way to church in Caterham.

But war approached. As 3 September 1939 came closer the working atmosphere became charged with the developing crisis. I was on duty overnight on 2/3 September and talked on the teleprinter with my operator colleague in the Central Telegraph Office and learned of the severance of all telegraphic links with Berlin twelve hours before the Chamberlain broadcast of war declaration. That day seemed to wear on with an almost tactile overcast of apprehension. We had already gained an armed policeman on duty at the entrance to the building. I went home to Tatsfield full of foreboding and the first air raid siren had already sounded. It was a false alarm but it tended to crystallise the awful situation.

I had begun to motor-cycle back and forth between Tatsfield and Caterham daily. The black-out came into immediate effect; the motor-bike's headlamp was masked and petrol rationing began. I was in a reserved occupation in communications and was able to secure extra petrol coupons; this 'reserved' occupation protected me from call-up to the Armed Forces. The staff at the office had already been depleted by pre-war mobilisation of reservists and by conscription. The HVP drop-kicker went to the Royal Signals in the first wave of conscription and served in France, East Africa, the Western Desert, Italy, the D-day landings. He also participated in the campaign to Lüneberg Heath where he was a player in the setting-up of the signals system for the signing of the German surrender.

The profound blow of Dunkirk in 1940 came and went and pretty soon thereafter there appeared a memorandum on the notice board to the effect that my grade of civil servant could join the Armed Forces by volunteering for flying duties with the Royal Air Force or the Fleet Air Arm. Immediately after my eighteenth birthday in 1940 I signed up for the RAF and later that year was summoned to Weston-super-Mare for two days of medical and general proficiency tests. I was accepted and celebrated in the station buffet at Bristol Temple Meads with a large, poor quality, sherry; the awful taste indicated it had been waiting for me to come for some time!

The Battle of Britain had begun and Tatsfield was in the midst of it. The direction of take-off of Spitfires and Hurricanes from Biggin Hill took them exactly over the village at low-level and maximum engine-power. Similarly, the noise of the inward high-level passage of German bomber and fighter daylight formations over Biggin Hill and into London airspace brought us close to the action. I witnessed many dogfights over the village and on one occasion saw twelve twin-engined Heinkel bombers go into a defensive circle and undergo attack by RAF fighters. One by one the enemy went down. Early in that air battle a Spitfire dived through the centre of the circle of Heinkels and went straight into the ground. The depleted enemy formation eventually broke up when the remaining aircraft dived away to take their own chances of escape. The sight and sound of these activities defies description – it was awe-inspiring and profoundly disturbing. When the night bombing of London began we took refuge in the home-made dug-out of a friendly customer-family nearby when the activity was at its height. Very obviously I never for a moment imagined that I would be deeply involved in a reversed role over Germany and Occupied Europe, nor did I fully appreciate the awful sound of a really heavy night bomber attack until I heard Royal Air Force night attacks in strength passing over my Gestapo prison cell in Brussels in late 1943. At that time it was a truly awful sound but, nevertheless, greatly encouraging.

But I must not stray into the future and should record that my father, as a Home Guard Lieutenant platoon commander, rescued a facially burned German fighter pilot from threatening Tatsfield farmworkers during the height of daylight attacks, before taking him prisoner. The young man was badly injured and went away in an ambulance.

In mid-May 1941 I received call-up documents instructing me to report on 4 August to the Air Crew Reception Centre in Hall Road, St Johns Wood (ACRC and known as 'Arsy Tarsy'). Early in the run-up period to call-up I spent a few days holiday with Aunt Lizzie Thomas at her house at Hove and saw Mary there. We had first met as small children for our families were connected by a marriage – that of Aunt Lizzie (my maternal grandmother's sister) and Uncle Tom Thomas, the family money-lender. Tom's cousin was Mary's father – both 100 per cent Welshmen. Soon after we met each other again at Lizzie's house at Hove I proposed under the railway-arch of the single line railway Brighton to Devil's Dyke. It was the beginning of the best years of our lives, although naturally there were bad patches. I had fallen for Mary's good looks and her charm, her courage, conviction and honesty. I stole her from a Captain in the Royal Artillery. I had my best stroke of good luck ever. The motor cycle was sold and the engagement ring bought with the proceeds!

At this point and before going further with the narrative it may be useful to gather thoughts on my beliefs, values and state of mind. Did I believe in anything, was I prepared to make the effort to respond totally to all the demands that might be made on me? – I had never exerted myself that way before – did I have any ambition to succeed or was I just shambling forward in the usual way? The answers at that time must have been that nothing much had changed within me since school. I had certainly been pretty conscientious in continuing studies for the Executive Grade in the Civil Service, but the need for this had been snuffed out at the outbreak of war when all Civil Service examinations were cancelled. The urge had been there to do the job so that was a plus. But I do not believe, in honesty, that there were any other pluses. Joining up was an act in tune with the war situation and I really did not have a resolution in me to press forward with a mission for success.

But what about the development of the psyche? Had I any deep feelings about anything? The answer must be in the affirmative. My developed feelings covered two areas. First I knew that I loved Mary. Secondly, I was a country boy and many precious impressions of country life were there and that was about the lot. I went forward blindly into change and to war, very moderately streetwise.

CHAPTER 4

Royal Air Force Training

The Royal Air Force Air Crew Reception Centre, a short distance from Lords Cricket Ground and Regents Park, was made up of large blocks of flats which had been taken over for Air Ministry use. They were thick on the ground and most were commandeered to serve the influx of Royal Air Force recruits. All the rooms were stripped of furniture and hangings and one slept on a mattress laid on the floor. All activity for that first fortnight was basic. We took our meals in the large restaurant in the Zoological Gardens which meant marching there and back three times a day. As the queues of 'flights' of fifty men moved slowly along Regents Park Road to the entrance of the Zoo and thence to the Restaurant, we were unfailingly greeted, barracked and urged on by the yelling of the caged monkeys – on some days their cries seemed derisive and mocking. We gathered uniforms, inoculations, identity cards and advice on how to avoid venereal disease, together with other items of airman's wisdom and necessity.

One incident lifted my confidence quite considerably. The intake included a Junior Station Inspector of the Metropolitan Police, a markedly pompous and objectionable individual whose special ability was to make the point that he was superior to everyone else. Then came the day when inoculations were to be administered to us all and this 'superior' being was immediately in front of me in a queue to stand before the doctor with the hypodermic. When his turn came he stepped forward, looked at the doctor and passed out on the floor! The knowledge that he had a marked weakness got around very quickly, giving rise to some moderate satisfaction that he had come down to earth!

My intake of about fifty men consisted mostly of ex-policemen who had volunteered, as I had done, in order to break out of a reserved occupation. My room-mates were two Metropolitan Police-men – Roy Evans and Alan Cordon; John Gerry, a Ph.D (Chemistry) and a laboratory assistant from Bootle, Alan Dickinson. Our intake was called 'A Flight' and marching drill began in the roads of St Johns Wood. I began to drink that odious elixir called 'Youngers Scotch Ale' and got gently drunk for the first time at the Sussex Arms in the West End of London.

A posting to the Initial Training Wing (ITW) at Torquay followed at the end of fourteen days and we entrained from Paddington, uniformed, equipped with identity cards and all those personal things that support smart cadet-airmen.

A sorting out took first place in the programme at Torquay: we had a clear month of concentration on mathematics and trigonometry. There was an examination and our comrade Alan Cordon failed. Sadly, he was posted back to his job in the police. The remainder went into the initial training proper and we learned how to receive and transmit in Morse Code, to operate, dissemble and reassemble a Lewis gun, the basics of navigation in Torbay, strategy and tactics in military affairs. There was much marching and one's own personal control, from time to time, of the fifty-man Flight, which I relished.

Finally, I found, as generations had done before me, that RAF/NAAFI tea is genuinely foul! Nonetheless, I enjoyed it all and formed a happy bond with Roy Evans, John Gerry and Alan Dickinson.

By early December we were ready to move on. Examinations had been passed and we were promoted Leading Aircraftsmen, given two weeks leave and ordered to return to Torquay before 2359 hours on the 14th day thereafter. I believe we had already become different people after the Royal Air Force initial training treatment and I began to feel good. I had achieved something and felt proud about it. I wanted other events to come on quickly for an urge had been awakened, as had a clearly formed purpose.

I spent all that fortnight with Mary, at Tatsfield and Brighton. In a vain attempt to make my home at Tatsfield smarter than it really was, I dismantled the lavatory seat in the 'loo-in-the-cupboard' and subjected it to a fierce sandpapering! Love demands extraordinary action! All too soon we parted at Paddington and I went on to Torquay again. News came immediately that we were to be shipped to South Africa for flying training within the Empire Flying Training Scheme.

To await this event we were moved to a transit centre in Heaton Park, Manchester where we were issued with tropical gear (including sun helmets) and awaited departure for South Africa.

I took the opportunity to suggest to Mary that she should come up to Manchester for a weekend, a plan to which she readily agreed. Panic developed between the two mothers and in the end they came up with her and stayed at the Midland Hotel. A clever move to sabotage any hanky panky had been devised in which they were completely successful! They probably celebrated their success too heartily for, when they returned to their room during one evening, my mother could not understand why the bathroom was so small – she had inadvertently stepped into the wardrobe!! However, the weekend was a success as Mary and I were together and the two mothers had bumped into Richard Tauber (an operatic heart-throb of the day) in the Midland Hotel.

We entrained and went northwards and boarded HM Troopship *Scythia* from a quayside somewhere on the Clyde in late November 1941. With a pronounced lump in my throat we quit the quay and passed down river to join a convoy in the northern Irish Sea. As Royal Air Force aircrew cadets we wore white flashes in our caps and were lucky to be favoured by the allocation of small four-bunk cabins. It was solely a trooping convoy, made up of well-known requisitioned passenger liners converted for troop-carrying.

After four days at sea and well into the Atlantic and the routine of the ship, we were at breakfast when the news came down to the mess-deck that the ship had fallen out of the convoy.

There had been a serious engine failure. The speed seen from the deckrail confirmed our plight: one propeller was turning very slowly, the other had stopped. We were making two knots at best and were an excellent U-boat target right in their front garden. A distant destroyer was signalling to us by Aldis lamp, a message which we hoped was 'Good Luck' – we needed it.

The Officer Commanding Troops advised us that, fortunately, Royal Navy engineers were on the ship and would assist with the repairs. He reminded all on board of our difficult situation. An immediate tightening up of ship abandonment drill followed. The lifeboats were already swung out as was customary when at sea in wartime. The personal prayer mats were in widespread use when retiring for the night! We were five thousand Army, Navy and Air Force personnel aboard and one civilian, Evelyn Baring, going out to Rhodesia, eventually to a Governorship.

Seven days or so passed before full power was restored to both engines. During this period there were two U-boat night alarms when any engine movement was halted, the ship was completely silent, had lost all forward momentum and rolled in the swell. The ship's company held its breath.

In seven more days of sailing at all possible speed we went into Freetown, Sierra Leone. *Scythia* had caught up with the convoy and we had much for which to be thankful.

Information released after the war revealed that HM Troopship *Lancastrian* was lost after an enemy torpedo attack. (This ship was not in our convoy, but it reminds me of our good fortune.) She had five thousand troops, other personnel, civilians and crew aboard and there were very few survivors. *Scythia* carried a similar number of souls aboard.

Christmas 1941 was upon us and was celebrated in Freetown with the ship lying in mid-river in high temperatures and heavy humidity. I watched the sweat drip off the nose of one of the ship's cooks and fall straight into my messroom's dish of turkey! I did not disclose that we had an additional amount of gravy but I remembered dear old Miles, the Tatsfield milkman, whose nasal aim was similar!

We spent most of the days on deck, watching the other ships at anchor, the activity around them and the local Sierra Leonian boys diving from their dug-out canoes for coins thrown by those richer than ourselves. One soldier leaned so far over the deck-rail that his sun helmet fell into the water. It was offered back to him for £5. The offer was turned down in terms that only a British Army squaddie can conjure up! The unloading of general supplies was watched intently, as they included quantities of canned beer; during the lowering of one large pallet a mishandling took place: the whole load was tipped into the waiting barge and all the cases broke open, depositing their contents into a monster heap of McEwans Best Export! There were loud cheers from the military spectators – made more in envy than derision. My education continued: up to that moment I had never heard of McEwans!

The convoy put to sea two days ahead of us. We rejoined it steaming alone at about 14 knots for what seems now to have been about six days. The convoy's escort had been strengthened and our place was a little astern on the port quarter of an aircraft carrier. The next port of call after a score of bingo games was Cape Town. It was a relief to arrive and a thrill to see Table Mountain and find the liners

Queen Mary and *Queen Elizabeth* in port, painted battleship grey overall. Within two weeks, including days ashore in Cape Town, we disembarked at Durban after a welcome from 'The Lady in White' on the jetty at the port entrance. Our group moved inland to Clairwood, the Durban racecourse, which had been converted into a giant Imperial Forces Transit Camp and we waited there for transfer to an Air Training School.

The period at Clairwood was long enough to spend some time in the city of Durban, see our first rickshaws and for Roy Evans to lose his single false tooth and to recover it in the sand in the nick of time on the morning of departure! We quit Durban and proceeded by train to the South African Army's Littleton Military Depot, lying between Pretoria and Johannesburg. Here we found out very soon that our presence in the country did not entirely please everyone. That issue apart, on arrival at Littleton we were delivered to the centre of the parade ground, having carried our total kit some distance from the railway station. An immediate haze of cigarette smoke appeared over our heads but within seconds after the light-up a frenzied scream of anger from a South African Sergeant-Major catapulted us into a state of shock and attention.

'How dare you smoke on my parade ground!'

Some punishing marching drill followed at once, given half in English and half in Afrikaans. We came later to like the man and greatly to respect him. Some South Africans took their nationalistic dislike to extremes and a few of our colleagues were beaten up by the Ossiewe Brandwag, the militant Afrikaner society. I was still learning about life and its potential for brutishness.

After some vigorous physical training at Littleton and leave in Pretoria and Johannesburg, we moved on to No. 42 Air School at Queenstown in the Eastern Cape Province. It was a South African Air Force airfield with a Royal Air Force training unit installed and officered by RAF personnel in the main, with some South African pilots, instructors and ground crews. Our course numbered fifteen cadets, all of whom had been together since St John's Wood.

We began to read Dead Reckoning and Astro Navigation, Meteorology, Maps and Charts, Instruments and Compasses, Photography and the theory and practice of Air Bombing. We flew in Avro Ansons, the old workhorses, for practical navigation instruction and Airspeed Oxford aircraft for air bombing practice covering, *in toto*, the greater part of Central and Eastern Cape Province in the process. Some of our navigational exercises took us over the great diamond hole at Kimberley which really is enormous and the Orange River – almost dry. We flew down to and over Port Elizabeth and East London *inter alia*. The ground was brown and dry and difficult to map-read and I quickly learned that air navigation is 98 per cent boredom and 2 per cent absolute terror. Our navigation instructor, Flight Lieutenant Peter Dickens, was a Master Mariner who brooked no nonsense. Accordingly, when he asked where I reckoned our aircraft was during a training flight, my mind seized up.

'You're smack on track at Burgersdorp, you idiot!'

About a third of the way through the thirteen week course two of our classmates were lost. One of the Ansons flew into a hill at Somerset East and all were killed. We were severely shaken, slow-marched at the funeral and witnessed the burials in the Queenstown Cemetery.

On return to the classroom Peter Dickens reminded us that we were now 13 strong, our course was No. 13 and that the next navigational exercise was on Friday the 13th of the month! He flew with us in one of the aircraft on that day.

I grew fond of Queenstown itself and will always associate it with the table-top mountain, Hangklip, which dominates its backdrop and the whole northern panoramic view. In those days it was a small town with a hexagonal central plaza and six roads radiating straight out of town, an arrangement designed to provide direct lines of fire when it was needed in earlier days.

Our contacts with the good people of Queenstown had been growing happily and following the accident they were cemented. The vicar, Canon Harold Rolfe, and his wife (a doctor) became friends with cadets throughout the whole series of war-time training courses. Hospitality went much further on occasions. Halfway through the course we were granted a long weekend leave and accepted an invitation to spend it on a sheep farm at Molteno, several hours train ride to the north of Queenstown, with a Mr and Mrs Pringle.

I learned here that the native uneducated shepherds could, easily and accurately, count the large numbers of sheep in their own way and check the result with Mr Pringle. He did not know their form of arithmetic and he had been a sheep-farmer for many years. Equating his method with that of his shepherd must have been interesting.

Our performance in practical target bombing was pathetic and towards the end of the course we were threatened with course failure if we did not improve substantially. We did qualify but could and should have done better. It is vital that the communication between bomb-aimer and pilot, in these exercises, should be by an intercommunication system, but Queenstown's aircraft lacked that facility. The pilot had to watch the legs of the student bomb-aimer during the run up to the target. Accuracy goes out of the window when reliance is placed on a left or right leg waggling about to indicate small changes in the heading of the aircraft! Left or right instructions on a bombing run are necessary as the aircraft goes forward and the target moves down the bombsight line in the instrument. When the point is reached where the markings on the instrument indicate the aircraft is 'on target' the bomb cargo is dropped. At that point the pressing of a button by the bomb-aimer activates each bomb release mechanism in the bomb bay. We were as much concerned with the problem of bombing accurately as we were with another issue.

Rumours were circulating at a rampant rate that the packing of parachutes was not being executed properly. The skilful packing procedure of these items was supervised by a South African Air Force corporal. The stories insisted that our parachutes were not reliable and, indeed, that a cadet had accidentally pulled his parachute open on the ground only to find that a bed blanket fell out! The corporal packer heard of this nonsense and demanded of the Commanding Officer that he be allowed to test his own packing by baling out over the airfield. This he did and killed the rumours stone-dead; his stock soared immediately with every cadet.

The end of No. 42 Air School course examinations revealed that our group of thirteen all qualified to move on to the next training phase – air gunnery. There had been some narrow escapes as a result of low examination marks for photography. This was very surprising for the sergeant instructor had made the nature of each question very clear before the examination. In so doing his keenness to be shown as a good and popular instructor was also monumentally obvious. Unfortunately some of us could not have been listening and made a near calamitous horlicks of their finals! I had scored an AA rating, having achieved an overall average marking of 80 per cent. I had never been in such a success position in my life before, in spite of making a bit of a pig's ear of the Maps and Charts examination. I felt better for my performance, for the first time in my life.

We moved down to the coast to Port Alfred at the mouth of the small River Kowie. The Airspeed Oxford aircraft used were fitted with a gun turret midway down the topside of the fuselage. One sat in the seat and bodily swivelled the turret in the direction of the target drogue before aiming and firing. The first time I climbed into the turret in the air I had to manoeuvre my six-foot frame into the seat by partly exposing my head to the aircraft slipstream. My flying helmet was whisked off and I got into trouble from the pilot for shooting at it as it fell away from the aircraft into the Indian Ocean! What was I then to do having lost my helmet? My friend John Gerry, six feet two inches, came to the rescue and put his arm through the window of the equipment store and 'selected' a new one!

The gunnery course was a doddle and I was pleased to have got away with a pass; I had the strongest feeling that I did not puncture the drogue target very much – but I did pass as a proficient air gunner. The examiners had to be right!

The end of the course at Port Alfred was the end of our training under the Empire Flying Training Scheme. The sixty cadets that had come out from UK on the *Scythia* were brought together from different training schools and paraded on the hangar tarmac apron for a passing-out ceremony. To my profound surprise I was the second most successful cadet of sixty examinees. An Air Commodore pinned on our brevet flying badges and, when I stood before him (a six foot four inch giant), he said, 'Harris, well done! We have recommended you for a commission and we usually get our way. Good luck.'

It had never occurred to me that I would be considered for such a recommendation. There were, I believe, four of us so recommended out of sixty men. It was quite a jump from Leading Aircraftsman to Pilot Officer. The commission warrant is dated 7 June 1942. It came into my possession fifty years later after I reminded the Ministry of Defence that it had never been issued.

The most successful cadet, Trevor Herbert, remained a sergeant and was killed on flying operations. He was very bright and a very likeable, retiring sort of chap with a very strong Herefordshire accent. It definitely should not have done, but I wondered whether this accent tipped the scale away from a recommendation for a commission.

We had all been issued with sergeant's stripes but I was immediately instructed not to wear them. When we all got drunk at the local hotel it did not seem to matter to anyone that I wore no stripes: we all got absolutely sloshed! Thereafter, of course, it did matter.

We travelled by train to Cape Town where I was kitted out with a Simpson of Piccadilly-built uniform and boarded HM *Samaria* into officers' accommodation. His Majesty's troopship *Samaria* was about to return to UK and would make the voyage unescorted. I was separated from my friends.

Samaria made 16 knots and I do not remember a stop between Cape Town and Liverpool. The anti-aircraft guns were manned by all ranks. The gun emplacements were egg-cup shaped positions which one reached by climbing over the deckrail and ascending a ladder into each gun platform. I did not enjoy the job at night and wondered, apart from torpedo track-spotting, what use any one of us could be with a single Lewis gun.

The voyage passed quickly and pleasantly. We disembarked at Liverpool, where I entrained to an Officers' Transit Unit at Bournemouth and from thence home on three weeks' leave. I felt the same lump in my throat at Liverpool on arrival, as in December 1941 when we quit the Clyde.

I arrived in Brighton in mid-July having been kept for just two days in the Transit Unit, a group of commandeered hotels in the general area of Christchurch Road in Bournemouth. During that time Mary had taken steps to secure a special marriage licence for a ceremony in Preston Old Church in Brighton.

The South Coast, including Brighton, was a prohibited area with policemen at all road and rail access points. No visitors were allowed in with the exception of residents' relatives. On the wedding day, I received the guests at Preston Park Station and weakly explained to the police constable that each visitor was a cousin; as each train discharged one or two more guests the officer on duty murmured politely: 'More cousins, Sir?'

He was a sympathetic man and my uniform helped.

My fellow RAF aircrew cadet, John Gerry, was best man and Mary's much treasured friend, Dorothy (Bubbles), from school-days was bridesmaid.

Our wedding reception took place at one of the hotels on Brighton sea-front. I certainly cannot remember details of the wedding 'breakfast' (as it was known in those days) with one exception: the luncheon started off with ice-cold soup – an unheard of dish at the time – and perhaps the guests may have thought that the hotel's cooking facilities had run into difficulties!

The whole event was put together in short order and ten days remained for a honeymoon. This was spent at the unlikely resort of Ilfracombe – in the apartment of Mary's Aunt Daisy. We had to wash in the kitchen sink (there being a dearth of bathrooms in the building) and we occupied some time cooking the food bought in the local grocer's shop – rationing was in full spate for sure.

There was a large Minton china piece representing St George and the Dragon gracing Daisy's sideboard and when she died many years later she willed it to Mary. It was a piece Mary greatly treasured, but in 1995 some thieving persons stole it during a daylight break-in at our home. The long arm of the lawless reached out and took an irreplaceable possession from us. I hope it brought them trouble and none of it trivial.

Just before I was due back from leave I sent a telegram to Bournemouth seeking an extension of my leave. No joy: the reply came quickly instructing me to report to the Advanced Navigation Training Unit at Dumfries. A railway travel warrant awaited me when we returned to Brighton. We were a little over twenty years of age and very happy, but within a year our world would change and we would both be put to the severest of tests by the brutality of war. Whilst flying in South Africa had been interesting, it was just the prelude to a very serious business. The start was the posting to Dumfries, to Number 10 (Observer) Advanced Flying Training Unit which concentrated on navigation at night and I served there for a month. I was now completely separated from my friends. Roy Evans and John Gerry were, like myself, somewhere in the United Kingdom whilst Alan Dickinson had left us in South Africa to be posted north for operational flying in the Mediterranean theatre of the war.

I experienced a standard of flying conditions and navigational performance in Scotland that was testing. I flew with a different pilot on each of the exercises. The black-out over the whole of Britain was complete and offered the student navigator no help. I look back on those days and wonder how the hell I found Barnard Castle and other comparable small towns in the dark – and then made it back to Dumfries airfield with that large natural mound, Criffel, so dangerously close to the airfield.

On one occasion I returned to Dumfries, flying with a sergeant pilot, and found that the base was shut in by fog. We decided to fly westward and try coming down over the sea beyond Stranraer. I timed our descent where I estimated we should be over the water. The descent was a nerve-wracking business and when we broke the cloud base we were directly over the port – a narrow escape. It had been our intent to fly back to base eastward along the coast but fuel was low. Accordingly, we adopted an alternative plan and flew low northwards, over the coastline to Turnberry airfield. We fell into that haven with a giant gasp of relief and very little fuel left in the tanks.

The next morning after refuelling we returned to Dumfries to be greeted with a very grim reception. The sergeant, as aircraft captain, had neglected to call the base through Flight Control – a serious error – and I had failed to remind him to do so. It was a first division shaker, the worst I had that far. I was not sorry to leave Dumfries: the quality of the pilots concerned me and there was a low level of navigational advice and back-up generally.

There was an exception: in leaving I lost the services of my first officer-servant – a batwoman. She was a red-headed Scots girl who took her duties very seriously, so much so that she would batter on my door in the early morning, march in smartly, seize me by the shoulder and shake me vigorously until I regained consciousness! It was fierce treatment. She also pressed every item of my uniforms as they had never been pressed before!

Dumfries itself did have one special quality. It was the home of the farming family Rogerson, whose younger daughter, Dorothy, had been Mary's special school-friend in London; she had recently returned to Bearcroft, the family farm, from our wedding. I met her future husband, George Carmichael, there in August 1942 when I was walking back from Bearcroft with Dorothy to the bus stop for Dumfries town. George caught up with us on his bicycle – a 'she-bike' – and after shaking hands threw the machine over the nearest hedge before walking the rest of the way with us. What a way to treat a bike, I thought, but the lady's machine still survives in one of the wings of his house.

Now George and I take turn and turn about to speak with each other every weekend to this day. He is a very senior retired magistrate, prominent local government figure and prison visitor in Dumfries and Galloway – and a good judge of a dram, especially if it is a 'doch an doris' – the penultimate drink.

Very sadly, Dorothy died in 1992. She taught me to say, with the local accent: 'Ha' ye nae got y' wumman w' ye?' (Haven't you got your woman with you?)

My next posting was to Upper Heyford where I reported to the Adjutant of No. 16 Operational Training Unit in September 1942.

It was here that the confluence of the various aircrew trades was centred. Aircraft crews were formed: pilots, navigators, bomb-aimers, flight engineers, radio operators and air-gunners flowed in from the Commonwealth and other Allied countries from all points of the compass. This gathering engineered for itself the formation of six-man crews. The system worked and quite soon in the mess, I, an observer/navigator, met Flying Officer (at that time) Colin Taylor, a pilot, who had come to Heyford from a Training Command Unit at Jurby on the Isle of Man. We talked about joining forces and quickly agreed to begin forming a crew. Immediately following is a short account of the coming together of the crew, an effective *laisser faire* function.

Whilst walking back to the Officers' Mess for lunch one day I met a section of aircrew men marching toward me. I immediately recognised my good friend Roy Evans among them. We shouted to each other:

Harris: 'Have you got a crew yet?'

Evans: 'No, but I've got an air-gunner. Have you got a pilot?'

Harris: 'Yes. Shall we get together?'

Evans: 'Right.'

This opportunistic flash of conversation was very necessary as it saw the beginnings of the foundation of a crew.

All aircrew, in training or not, had been advised of a new classification of aircrew trades. The need for change had been brought about by the advent in great numbers of four-engined aircraft in Bomber Command, necessitating the abolition of the Observer trade. Observers had performed in the roles of navigator, bomb-aimer, air gunner and map-reader in all twin-engined aircraft. Now, save for the new twin-engined De Havilland Mosquito, the larger four-engined Avro Lancaster, Handley Page Halifax and Short Stirling needed individual operatives. Thus were introduced the 'N' flying badge for navigators, 'E' for Flight Engineer, 'B' for Bomb-aimer and 'AG' for Air Gunner. The Wireless Operator wore 'AG' with a radio insignia on an arm badge. For men like Roy Evans, who had trained and qualified as navigators, this change to 'B' was a disappointment. He had done excellently in navigational training and would have felt downgraded as Bomb Aimer. However, in the nose of any aircraft Roy was a consummate aimer and a brilliant guide and map-reader. I was lucky to be classified navigator and to get Roy in my crew in his changed trade and, furthermore, doubly fortunate to keep him as a friend for over fifty-seven years. I never replaced my own 'Observer' badge with an 'N' on my uniforms.

As I had already met Colin Taylor and had agreed with him to team-up, we officially registered our intent to form a crew. We confirmed our intent with Roy and Ronnie Chisholm, a rear-gunner from Seattle. Colin had secured Douglas Inggs as Wireless Operator, having known him at Jurby. So we were almost set up, save for a Flight Engineer. Cecil Anderson (Andy), a Canadian, joined us a little later as a Flight Engineer. Both Chisholm and Anderson were with the Royal Canadian Air Force.

Ronnie Chisholm had worked for Boeing in Seattle having won a world-wide aircraft modelling competition, part of the prize for which was a job with Boeing. Cecil Anderson was serious and purposeful and at twenty-seven years of age was the 'old man' of the crew.

Flying began in twin-engined Wellington aircraft. I felt comfortable with our arrangements, the more particularly because of Colin's very many hours of pilot experience on twin-engined Hampden bombers in Training Command.

The flying programme commenced on 10 October and ended on 26 November 1942. We flew in Wellington Marks 1 and 3 aircraft, the latter being a development of the basic Wellington type fitted with Bristol Hercules radial engines. Clearly they were powerful units and the aircraft was one in which the crew enjoyed flying. For my part I felt the surge of power and compared it with the noisy 'Cheetah' engine of the Avro Anson.

The operational training course consisted of daylight navigational exercises, in the main, combined with bombing practices. We returned from one bombing practice to be told that we had been very successful. The target in the Severn Estuary had been hit and comprehensively destroyed.

'You are not supposed to destroy the bloody target!' we were told. Full marks to Roy Evans.

The last exercise was a night flight during which we had to make a bombing run on Goole, near Hull, coming from the east to a target infra-red lamp in the centre of the town. Success was measured on an exposure of photographic film in an aircraft camera and I believe we achieved it. This was our last flight of the programme and the crew had come together very well, each being able to show his proficiency to the comfort of the others.

Mary and I celebrated our twenty-first birthdays in Oxford (with Colin on one occasion), by having tea at the Randolph Hotel.

Three other incidents within the period of our time at Upper Heyford are worth recording. The first touches on the Hercules engines. As junior officers in the mess Colin and I and others were told one day that the station was about to entertain Lord Woolton, the Minister of Food and on the chosen date we were to take our meals in the Sergeants' Mess and to keep clear until the evening. When we returned, the Station Commander recounted the events of the day and told us that Lord Woolton had shown great interest in the aircraft we were flying. On being told of the Bristol Hercules radial engine equipment his Lordship commented:

'How interesting. They must be pretty good. My daughter bought a bicycle from them before the war.'

Certainly Hercules bicycles were popular amongst my generation, but his Lordship's pronouncement caused much derisive and disrespectful laughter.

The junior officers in the mess had to finish up the puddings left by the distinguished luncheon guests. They were very good: the rationing system must have been stretched to its limits to provide desserts of such quality for HM Minister of Food and other guests – and some senior Royal Air Force Officers.

The second incident was a tragedy. Soon after arriving at Upper Heyford I met an old school-friend from Oxted school-days who had completed pilot training and who had already formed a crew. I knew his parents and his siblings. A little later, on a night flight, his Wellington crashed in North Yorkshire and all the crew were killed. The Station Commander agreed that I should represent the Royal Air Force at his funeral at Limpsfield where his family lived. He lies close to the grave of Delius, the blind English composer. At the funeral his father said that he did not accept that his son, John, was capable of any pilot error and he intended to find out the cause of the crash in due time.

Ferguson Senior, a tough New Zealander and owning a prosperous electrical business, then embarked on a crusade to find out the cause of his son's death. He eventually did just that by bribing a staff member of the office in which accident records were kept. The crash was apparently caused by a technical fault in the aircraft itself. All this was revealed to me when I returned to the UK in 1945 by a father whose son had, in his view, been vindicated. The father had also traced John's Women's Auxiliary Air Force (WAAF) girl-friend and again confirmed other matters for himself. He was more than pleased by his son being cleared of responsibility for the fatal crash.

The third incident included my new wife, Mary. We arranged that she should come to Oxford for a weekend and I made a reservation at the Randolph Hotel. Upon our arrival we presented ourselves at reception to be greeted by a large-bosomed elderly lady in black. Hers was not a welcoming style.

'We have a reservation of a double room for two nights. My name is Harris.'

'This hotel does not provide rooms for young people like you whose purpose is very obvious.'

'I am afraid I do not understand.' Of course I got her drift.

'You should be ashamed of yourselves.'

At this point, in an attempt to prove that we were very respectable, Mary produced a tiny book of wedding photographs from her handbag and handed it over to the guardian of the morals of the Randolph Hotel.

'Oh dear, I am so sorry. We do have to be so careful, you know.'

We did not appreciate the apology.

Today we have three children and seven grandchildren and remain quite streetwise in the current scene.

In leaving Upper Heyford I lost the services of a batman, a long-serving member of that fraternity who was, at any time of day, properly attired in dark suit and highly polished brass crowns on both lapels of his jacket. He must have served scores of young officers like me, so it was not surprising to discover a man with a truly lugubrious mien.

Sandwiched between Upper Heyford and the next flying posting there was a three-week mandatory commando course to be taken by all aircrew. Apparently, at some point in the North African Desert War, it had been necessary to call in maximum armed manpower, including any available aircrew not currently flying. They were given weapons and placed in the defence lines. At the sight of the enemy tanks approaching they took a quick decision based on their not being engaged for land warfare: they bolted! Thereafter the Air Council decided that all aircrew should have their resolve stiffened by a commando course.

The Commanding Officer of the unit conducting the courses, a Squadron Leader, greeted us with the exhortation that we should work hard and play hard. I can faithfully claim that we did both very well. I specially enjoyed it all and came fourth in the seven mile road race in a reasonable time. Vigorous competitive games were played, walls were climbed, ditches were crossed and a hundred thunder flashes were thrown. Furthermore, the CO was carried up to his bed from the bar by members of the course every night we were there!

It was here that I came into close physical competitive contact with Denis Street, the son of the Permanent Secretary at the Air Ministry; he had been at Heyford but our courses separated us. He was to die as an escaper from Stalag Luft 3 at the hands of the Gestapo along with forty-nine other officers.

We reported to the last of our training units on 29 December 1942, for my part sixteen months after I first joined in August 1941. The crew was to be at 1654 Conversion Unit at Wigsley in the Midlands until early February, taking a full month to go through the process of change to a four engined aircraft and familiarisation with the Avro Lancaster.

We had first to deal with the Avro Manchester, an aircraft of ill-repute and the pre-cursor of the Lancaster. We had fourteen hours flying in Manchesters on cross-country trips and bombing practice on a target placed on the sand flats of the Wash off Wainfleet. Flights in Lancasters were made with Colin Taylor taking further conversion instruction, plus air gunnery firing.

At this point in our training we were joined by our last crew member, Billy Henderson (Geordie), our mid-upper turret air gunner, completing our seven-man crew.

On one occasion during our presence at Wigsley, the unit was called on to take part in the first 1000 bomber raid on Cologne. This

40

demand for maximum effort meant flying aircraft that were exposed to special stress in the crew conversion process: constant take-offs, circuits and landings. We did not fly as a crew on this trip and during a walk around some of the aircraft dispersal points I saw Mickey Martin and talked with him as he cleaned the windshield of his aircraft. Colin, Mickey and I shared a bedroom for three in the accommodation block. He (Martin) and others became famous as Dam Busters in 617 Squadron in 1943. He and I were to meet again much later in our lives.

A crew of our friends did not return from this operation, a group of seven men with whom we had trained since Upper Heyford days; Colin and I felt this particular loss very keenly. The pilot was a friendly fellow called Stockwell, the bomb aimer a one-time Inspector in the Rhodesian police named John Leonard and the navigator Gwyn Morgan. Leonard and Morgan were utterly different types. The former, much the elder by ten or twelve years, carried a photograph in his wallet which he delighted in showing anyone whom he thought he could shock. It concerned his first case of suicide and the picture was of a man with the top of his head blown off. Gwyn Morgan was a musician and at fourteen years of age had been one of the assistant organists at Westminster Abbey at the Coronation of George VI. I saw and heard him play a piano sonata in the Mess at Heyford and was profoundly struck by the passion with which he played the piece – his character was so far removed from dropping bombs in anger. What a loss and how much our cultural future was depleted by brutal and vicious events. We understood they went down into the North Sea on the return leg of the mission.

The course at 1654 Conversion Unit kept us fully occupied. I had to do a stint as Orderly Officer and on one occasion performed the function jointly with a WAAF Officer. In her travels through the cookhouse she found it necessary to descend into the cellars wherein was stored the coal. Unfortunately when she reached the cellar floor she disturbed a Warrant Officer and a WAAF performing earnestly and sexually on the coal heap! Surely they would have been more comfortable almost anywhere else and, I wonder, whatever happened to the Warrant Officer – or the girl?

It was at this station that I had a tussle with a Warrant Officer in charge of the cookhouse. I appeared with an Orderly Sergeant at a mealtime in the airmen's mess to answer the traditional call: 'Attention! Orderly Officer! Any complaints?'

An airman stood up and complained and showed me a meat pie which had green mould under the pastry. We repaired to the kitchen and met the Warrant Officer. The offending pie was revealed to him and he retired behind some ovens to attend to the problem. He returned to me carrying the plate and I had him lift the pastry from the top of the pie. It was obviously the same pie covered with a flood of gravy. I said: 'Don't bugger me about, Mister, change this airman's meal at once and completely.' If he had a soup ladle in his hand he would have come close to striking me! It pleased the airman and impressed the Orderly Sergeant no end. I did not hear any more sotto voce comments, when I returned the next day – such as: 'He's just a bloody sprog officer.'

Before I move on to the next posting I will record that in the bar of the Officers' Mess at Wigsley I witnessed, on a number of evening occasions, the unusual use of a silk scarf. The Adjutant, whose name I do not recall and who claimed to be a literary man with a penchant for poetry, would put the scarf round his neck and push his right wrist through a loop at one end. As the evening passed he needed to pull the other end to lift the glass in his shaking right hand.

My education was certainly shaping up convincingly since joining the Royal Air Force. I had come a long way, literally and figuratively speaking, and I was positively aware of what I was doing and had some sense of what I had achieved. Commissioning had been a welcome surprise and I could now measure and appreciate how acceptable it was. In a motivated state of mind I felt good within myself, more generally concerned and reasonably confident. The annotation 'Above average navigator' in my flying log-book generally encouraged me then and much later in life when I had cause to undergo adversity

My crew was posted on 3 February 1943 to 50 Squadron, a pre-war squadron based at Skellingthorpe, very close to the City of Lincoln, on its western side. The task for which we had been trained was about to begin . . .

CHAPTER 5

Operational Flying

The Crew
Pilot: Flight Lieutenant Colin Taylor
Navigator: Pilot Officer Stewart Harris
Bomb Aimer: Sergeant Roy Evans
Flight Engineer: Sergeant Cecil Anderson RCAF
Wireless Operator: Sergeant Douglas Inggs
Mid-Upper Gunner: Sergeant Billy Henderson
Rear Gunner: Sergeant Ronnie Chisholm RCAF

Skellingthorpe airfield was a war-time airfield and a satellite of a larger, prewar Royal Air Force Station at Waddington. It lay immediately south of the road out of Lincoln south-westwards. The buildings were erected to accommodate the needs of war-time activity, all of one storey only with Nissen huts for all personnel accommodation on the opposite side of the Lincoln road. I cannot remember how we reached there from Wigsley but our arrival date was 3 February 1943.

The crew reported to the Squadron Flight Office, Colin Taylor and I also reporting personally to the Adjutant representing the Squadron Commander. The 'Adj' was a Flight Lieutenant Avis who wore an 'O' flying badge, indicating his trade as an Observer in much earlier flying days. In contemporary parlance he was laid back, extremely confident and I liked him immediately. We had begun to learn the ordered routine of squadron life. Our next call was the Officers' or Sergeants' Mess. We were soon welcomed personally by the CO Wing Commander Bill Russell, and his black Labrador dog.

The Squadron was made up of A and B Flights, each of 9 Lancaster aircraft. The crew became members of 'B' Flight led by Squadron Leader Peter Birch. 'A' Flight was led by Squadron Leader Douglas Street, later to become known as 'Pranger' Street when he got a Lancaster in a landing position much too high and just fell onto the runway!

We had become a small part of a very experienced unit, a top squadron. Three days later we were allocated an aircraft and made our

50 Squadron 1943.
L to R: Anderson, Harris, Evans, Taylor, Henderson, Inggs, Chisholm

first flight on '50', a squadron within 5 Group of Bomber Command. This first flight was a night flying test (NFT) prior to a training night flight where we were to pinpoint and record on our aircraft camera an infra-red light in the centre of Goole on the Humber. (As we had done previously, as mentioned in the last chapter.) Our approach was made from the North Sea against very accurate searchlight batteries and we reached the infra-red light with great difficulty. Our vigorous evasion of the searchlights, turning toward and through them as they came near, played havoc with our Dead Reckoning and gyro compasses causing the former to swing wildly and the latter to rotate continuously. Another NFT followed the next day when we practised evasive tactics against a 'hostile' Spitfire, turning into the line of attack to make it more difficult for the fighter pilot to get us into his gun sights.

That same night, 7 February, we flew to Lorient on the north-west coast of France to bomb the Atlantic U-boat pens with armour piercing bombs. It had taken eighteen months of training to drop the first bomb in anger.

This first operational flight was quite straightforward save for a tricky early incident. The flight began with a climb to operational height on a course of 190 degrees immediately after take-off. Twenty minutes later at 8000-9000 feet the aircraft began gently to lose height and to turn slowly to port. The problem quickly became more urgent but a solution was found swiftly by Cecil Anderson, the Flight Engineer, sitting alongside Colin Taylor. Colin's face mask connection to the oxygen supply had become detached and he was passing out for want of oxygen. Andy moved rapidly, reconnected the hose and kept the aircraft straight and level until Colin recovered. It was a little disturbing and quite a baptism on the first operation. The rest of the flight to the target was uneventful and we were not troubled by the anti-aircraft defences of Lorient. The balloons over the port area were clearly visible below us and our run-up was undisturbed and the return to base followed without incident – a flight-time of 5 hours 20 minutes. The cargo of armour piercing bombs was designed to penetrate the target's extensive submarine pens under considerable depths of concrete. Seven aircraft were lost by Bomber Command that night but our squadron was unscathed.

The routine of squadron operation was now clear. Whether or not the squadron had operated the night before, one reported to the Flight Office the next morning to find out whether anything was 'on' for the night; if so, and as soon as the aircraft was refuelled and ready, the crew took the aircraft on a short NFT to check all systems. After lunch we attended our appropriate aircrew trade leaders' meetings and then proceeded at 1600 hours for the main briefing. The squadron always operated at maximum strength. We learned the identity of the target, the tactics of the flight-timing, tracks and attack altitude, aiming points, intelligence and meteorological reports. As Navigator I marked my charts appropriately, collected my recognition codes book and returned to the mess for supper, usually a pleasant meal of eggs and bacon. The time always passed very quickly and in no time at all we boarded the aircrew bus to the aircraft dispersal point. I must concede that there were times when I hoped that by some fluke our crew would not be named on the operations board for the night. I always compared the feeling with the one I had when it became time to go back to school after a long summer's holiday, hoping that by some miracle an earthquake had swallowed the building, but the hope always evaporated. It was the same with

Reunion 1988. L to R: Evans, Anderson, Taylor, Harris, Inggs, Henderson.

an operational flight: as soon as I climbed into the aircraft the bad feeling disappeared and I got on with the job, from the beginning to the end.

Within a day or so of the trip to Lorient I attended a short instruction course on the new instrument called 'Gee', at that time a most secret piece of equipment, or so it was claimed. Its operation was simple and its ability to position the aircraft precise. Three co-ordinates showed on a round screen; the first and base line was the aircraft's position and the second and third represented the values of two radar signals. When in the air one read off the second and third co-ordinates against the base line on the screen and transferred these figures to the appropriate bearing line on a chart which was criss-crossed by lines bearing those values. Where those two lines crossed each other was one's position over the ground. It worked extremely well and I was able to win a fiver one day by saying that I could tell the crew, from behind my black curtain, when we would be exactly over the centre of our airfield. I enjoyed using 'Gee' over the UK but it was useless once one crossed the enemy coast. The Germans jammed it right out of play.

The next target on the night of 11 February was Wilhelmshaven, an important and well-defended German naval harbour on their North Sea coast. Again armour-piercing bombs were dropped from 20,000 feet. The attack was made from overland seaward. I recall my first experience of the accuracy of German anti-aircraft fire: as soon as we began flying straight and level on our bombing run the bursts of firing came closer with each shot until the aircraft jumped in response to the bursting shell. We came out of the target area very quickly! I still have the feeling that this Bomber Command effort was not a success. Three aircraft from the Command failed to return.

On 14 February we returned to Lorient. A two-wave attack was made and 1000 tons of explosives were dropped. The newspapers made much of the alleged success of the raid but the effort cost eight aircraft. We were back at base after a flight of 5 hours 25 minutes. My log-book records that we had a passenger, a Flight Sergeant Medani – a navigation instructor.

On 16 February we took off again for Lorient. My log book records that we returned to base after a three hour flight. I recall that we were having trouble with the engines which had been fitted with American Stromberg carburettors. The object of the Stromberg equipment was to overcome the effect of negative gravitation on fuel flow causing the loss of power in the engines when taking violent avoiding action. We found that when we brought in the superchargers at 12,000 feet the engines began to surge unreasonably causing severe loss of power. This problem caused us to return to base, after jettisoning our bomb load into the North Sea.

On 18 February I recorded a 90 minute daylight flight on which we carried two Rolls-Royce engineers (complete with leather elbow patches on their sports jackets – a sartorial sign of the times) to witness the behaviour of the Lancaster's Merlin engines when the superchargers were introduced. They made copious notes, with some satisfied excitement, and the problem of the irregularly surging engines was solved in short order.

That same night we went back to Wilhelmshaven. The briefing was explicit: we were to bomb from 21,000 feet, make a good straight and level run up to the dockyard aiming point and be especially accurate. There would be intense anti-aircraft fire and immediately after the drop we should get out of the area as quickly as possible. This did not mean that we should put the nose down and go back to base at low

47

level because the enemy had placed Flak-ships (anti-aircraft gun ships) at precisely the position where we might reach a low level. This would invite a welcome by searchlights and heavy and light anti-aircraft fire. An unhealthy place in which to loiter.

The weather was good, the target clear and the defence very accurate and active. We left the place very fast: so fast that I remember watching the wings shaking. The ideal height to level out would have been 8000 feet (it being the height recommended at briefing). But we went on descending and very shortly were caught in a searchlight and the flak started coming up at us. Colin put the nose of the aircraft down again but Roy yelled at him: 'Pull up for Christ's sake!' We narrowly missed diving into the sea and were so close that we lost our radio trailing aerial.

We were all pretty shaken by this episode. For my part, I found it calming to consume – unusually – all my flying rations which amounted to sandwiches, chewing gum, coffee, and a bar of chocolate. Unfortunately, I swallowed the chewing gum! During the return flight we received radioed instruction to 'BFX Bourne', which, when decoded, directed that we were to divert to Royal Air Force Bourne in Cambridgeshire (a Short Stirling aircraft base), because of bad weather at Skellingthorpe. Lancasters flew more swiftly than Stirlings so 50 Squadron was stacked up over Bourne at 500 feet intervals when the home-based aircraft began to arrive. We were not popular visitors that night. Four aircraft were lost by the Command on this operation.

A short return flight took us back to base the next morning where we learned that there was no flying that night. Roy Evans and I decided that we would go into Lincoln that evening for a meal and a couple of pints.

I had not felt fit since take-off from Bourne but decided that the outing would be a relaxation and a cure. There were not many eating places in the city in those days but we chose one and made our selection at the table. Hardly had we settled this part of the proceedings when I quietly passed out. Fortunately I was on a bench seat and conveniently went down along it. The restaurant management called an ambulance at the same time as Roy rang the Air Raid Precautions (ARP) base in the city and sought medical help. So, in a few minutes we had a choice and the ARP ambulance won. I was taken to a hospital and very closely examined. Nothing medically suspicious could be found. The Medical Officer was puzzled and advised that I go back to bed. His farewell question was: 'Have you been under stress very recently?' I do not remember my exact answer but I might well have shrugged a little and said: 'Could be.'

But that was not the end of this story. Two or three weeks later I received an invoice from the Lincoln City Corporation which required payment of one pound five shillings (£1.25) for the use of the Corporation's ambulance on the night of 19 February. I ignored it and eventually got notice of the issue of a writ if I did not pay within seven days. At this point wisdom took over and I went to the Adjutant for his advice and put the case to him. He immediately called the Town Clerk on the telephone, protesting that it was a bit rich to make such a charge to an officer on active service. The reply was:

'Would Pilot Officer Harris agree to pay five shillings?'

'Sounds reasonable,' said the Adj. 'I'll ask him.'

Adj: 'Will you pay five bob?'

Harris: 'Will they take a cheque?'

Adj: 'He will pay and he won't bugger about any longer!'

I got the message and paid up.

We flew to Nuremberg on 26 February in a force of 450 four engined aircraft. The Pathfinder Force (PFF), which was to mark the target with flares, was late and the most disorderly, horrific air traffic jam built up over the city as more and more main force aircraft arrived. When the flares went down every aircraft pounced on the target and dropped its bomb cargo. It must have been the height of terror and pandemonium on the ground. It was a chastening journey. Nine aircraft of the total force did not return.

On 28 February we were to attack targets at St Nazaire. My log-book records that we had to return to base without reaching the target. I cannot recall the reason but it must have been a good one. No questions were asked of us but a pretty objectionable guy called Trevor-Roper, later one of Guy Gibson's air-gunners, said: 'You ought to be considered as LMF!' (lack of moral fibre). I believe he was told to get stuffed or its equivalent in those distant days.

At this point, and being reminded of the issue of LMF, I recall that on 50 Squadron there were three cases whilst we were there. One was a young Pilot Officer whom I had met at Upper Heyford and who followed us to 50. He told me one day that he had just declared to the

CO that he could not undertake any more operational flights. He looked quite ashen.

The second was a Sergeant pilot who deliberately damaged his aircraft's cockpit essential flying control instruments in an attempt to avoid further flying against the enemy. This had happened once before in the pilot's position on this Sergeant's aircraft. He was court-martialled.

The third was a last minute refusal to fly by a pilot on the flight deck of an aircraft. The pilot was immediately replaced by the CO, Wing Commander Russell, who flew the operation in his shirt-sleeves. It was a Bomber Command full strength operation and Bill Russell's immediate reaction was to maintain full squadron strength and go himself. He was a true leader in a position of command.

Whilst on this subject, Max Hastings came to see me when he was writing his book on Bomber Command. He asked me whether it was true that there had been a camp in North East England specially to hold LMF cases. He had heard there were two thousand individuals there. I said I knew absolutely nothing of any such unit and doubted its existence.

We entered the briefing room on the afternoon of 1 March to be told by Bill Russell that: 'Tonight it's the Big City – Berlin.' This operation was to be the longest in flight time so far and one felt the weight and responsibility of such an effort.

The all-up weight of the aircraft was the highest ever, aggregating aircraft weight, bomb cargo and a full load of 100 octane gasoline fuel. There was to be an outward track to the Frisian Islands, thence to a point on the enemy's Baltic coast and then southwards to Berlin. Thereafter a short dog-leg track of 200 degrees and the long haul back to the Frisian Islands and back to base. Nineteen of the total aircraft despatched failed to return.

This trip was, for me, the most stressful so far and the sight of the city of Berlin burning and the remarkable accuracy of the defensive shooting were experiences I shall not forget. On such occasions I would get up from the navigator's seat, push aside for a moment the black curtain which shielded my navigation table spotlamp and 'Gee' screen from the flight deck; then I would stand for a minute or two watching the hellish scene unfolding below in this giant amphi-theatre.

It went smoothly for us but we saw other aircraft caught in

searchlights or being attacked by following Junkers 88 night-fighters. As RAF aircraft went down and no parachutes appeared, one wanted to scream: 'Get out of the bloody thing!'

With fires widespread in the city, one could see the shimmering of the locally heated atmosphere when 4000 lb. bombs hit the ground and when anti-aircraft fire was intense. The whole scene was a great theatre of drama, brutality, punishment, destruction and fire. We returned to base after 7 hours 10 minutes in the air – the time taken, today, to fly to New York by Boeing 747.

All members of a crew were awarded an issue of a colour print of a Lancaster where it could be proved from photographs taken at the moment of impact of the bomb-load that special accuracy had been achieved. We received such an award for this trip for which credit must flow to Roy Evans' bomb-aiming and Colin's piloting. We received several of these awards throughout our time at 50 Squadron.

The next day we did an altitude test on Lancaster 482 and reached a height of 28,000 feet. I was surprised how small the city of Leeds appeared from such a height but, of course, similar aerial views are now commonplace. At this point my log-book shows that for 21 days I did no flying; this must have been our first leave during a projected tour of 30 operational trips.

On our return we took over Lancaster 755 'Q' Queenie and kept her for the remainder of our time on 50. We took her to 25,000 feet on a Night Flying Test and that night took her to Berlin for our second visit. The flight to the city was different, very different. Our track from the east coast at Mablethorpe took us over the North Sea to the west coast of Denmark as close as possible to the surface of the water. The flight continued across that country at the same low level and, save for Colin, whose concentration on flying at this height was absolute, one could see, here and there, Danish folk outside their colour-washed houses watching and waving at the thunderously noisy airfleet going by just over their heads. This scene was not without its early tragedies. On first reaching the Danish coast one Lancaster made a mis-judgement and flew into the ground.

Further on the ground rose a little and I warned Colin and Roy of this hazard. We cleared it comfortably, but another Lancaster did not. It must surely have been caused by lack of watchfulness and a poor level of concentration by those at the front-end of the aircraft.

From the east coast we turned onto a course for Rostock and

climbed as fast as possible to the operational height of 20,000 feet whilst over the Baltic Sea. Shortly before reaching our turning-point at Rostock, a four-engined aircraft could be seen still flying very low beneath us, obviously not following the tactical briefing instructions. It was approaching a gaggle of small ships right in its path and was shot down instantly. Why did he not follow instructions?

Over Rostock we turned and set course southwards to Berlin. The scene at the target was a repeat one, but with a stronger red glow everywhere, plus much more defensive activity. Other bombing aircraft were so easily visible and all were targets for gun-fire and night-fighters. Once again, a dog-leg track out of Berlin airspace and back across Northern Germany; but things went badly wrong navigationally. On this course we were seriously adrift of our track. The pin-point on the North Sea coast did not show up. The night was black and we flew on until we could discern a coastline. As the navigator I was not able to detect any change in wind direction which would have caused such a long overshoot of the correct turning point.

Eventually, we found the continental coastline and entered southern English airspace at a point 90 miles from the correct landfall and we were, accordingly, late back to Skellingthorpe.

The following day I was called to the Navigation Leader's office to explain. I admitted that I should have done better in the circumstances despite the absence of stars for an astro-navigational shot with the bubble sextant and the ineffectiveness of 'Gee' over enemy occupied territory. I had failed to use my common sense on this leg and should have elected to turn north at as good an estimated point as possible and flown into the effective coverage of 'Gee' over the UK instead of going on to an identifiable coastline.

I got a very serious ticking-off for allowing my mind to freeze up. Our flight had taken 7 hours 2 minutes. Thirty-three more aircraft had been lost that night.

This incident was to haunt me for some time. It became a constant reminder to me always to look ahead and attempt to store up alternative actions should a crisis be developing.

It had dealt me a devastating mental blow by exposing my error.

For many years thereafter, when I made the tiniest of errors I experienced the same feeling of devastation in my mind.

It was 27 March that day and my birthday. Earlier in the day, when we were at the end of the runway on the point of starting our run for take-off for a Night Flying Test, there came a radio call from the Control Tower: Pilot Officer Harris was to leave the aircraft at once and report to the control tower immediately. The Lancaster was a hell of a distance from the Control Tower but I made it as quickly as possible, reaching the control room thoroughly out of breath. 'Blackie' (Flight Lieutenant Blackmore), the senior Flying Control Officer, came forward with a serious look on his face. It changed in a moment or so and he yelled at me: 'Happy birthday, Stew!' and gave me a telegram of greetings from Mary.

On 1, 2, and 3 April we carried out Night Flying Tests but no operations followed, suggesting that we were on readiness but weather over the target or unknown circumstances had ruled out ops. It must have been one of these nights when we were prepared enough to have reached the aircraft when the flight was 'scrubbed'. Ronnie Chisholm was very fed-up because he had already taken a heavy dose of caffeine tablets, to keep him awake during the flight. The next day he said he had enjoyed a very good night's sleep!

On 4 April we flew to Kiel. The newspapers said that the strength of the bombing force was the largest for four weeks and that many fires were started. Twelve aircraft did not return. My log-book does not record the incident but during the flight one of the pipes burst in the hydraulic system which operated the mid-upper turret. It had become inoperable and Billy Henderson was soaked in oil. He was alarmed at the drenching, thinking that somehow he had been hit. He had not and said, in Geordie language: 'Ah thowt it was bludd.'

Thereafter, and between 4 and 9 April, we were kept very occupied with practices involving fighter attacks from a friendly Spitfire and how to take avoiding action, dive testing the aircraft and bombing a specially built ground target in the Wash near Wainfleet.

On 9 April we flew to Duisberg and dropped the conventional bomb-load of one 4000 lb. 'cookie' and an assortment of 500 lb. bombs and canisters of incendiaries. On this trip we had a brush with a night-fighter whom our air-gunners Ronnie and Geordie sent away in a damaged condition. This was our claim at de-briefing.

My log-book does not record another incident, but I believe my memory is accurate. During the flight the forward gun turret, used by the bomb-aimer when required, sprang a leak in its hydraulic system. The oil sprayed back and covered the front windshield in front of the pilot. The wipers were used to very little effect. We made two attempts to land at base and had to abort each effort. 'Blackie', the Flying Control Officer, sent us away for twenty minutes instructing: 'Q Queenie, Johnson Johnson 20.'

This coded message ordered us to go away and not return for twenty minutes. On our return to the circuit and after three more tries we landed. The following moving and laconic dialogue ensued:

'Q Queenie pancaked – over and out' – the usual formula after a successful landing. Tower replied: 'Understood. You really are shockers – over and out.' Our flying time was 4 hours 45 minutes. Eight RAF aircraft did not return.

On 11 April we flew to Frankfurt. It was a failure. When we arrived at the target area, flying at 20,000 feet, the ground was completely covered by a blanket of cloud at 8000 feet. We dropped our bombs on a red area showing faintly through the cloud. Eight Bomber Command aircraft failed to return. We claimed a fighter shot down. The operation was a waste of time, lives and machines.

Our operations so far were bombing missions. The next was to be different. We flew to La Spezia on the west coast of the Italian mainland. The task was to lay sea-mines at the natural entry to the port which handled the Italian Navy and general shipping. The main force of 350 four engined aircraft was to bomb the ships and port installations, whilst 16 other aircraft, including 'Q' Queenie, were to lay mines in an attempt to sink ships as they fled the attack on the port by the main force. The briefing was detailed and specific. A very small island at the entrance to the bay was to be pinpointed and, flying at near zero feet, our sea mines were to be dropped at eight second intervals on a heading towards the precipitous coast with sheer cliffs much higher than we would be flying. Should we be fired on by a single light anti-aircraft gun on the island, we were to return the fire. It was alleged that the Italian gun crews were part-time operators, like the Home Guard at home – of whom it was alleged that, when fired upon, they would duck down below the parapet and desist!

This trip merits a more detailed description of what happened.

We flew south from Skellingthorpe to Dungeness and from thence to a point in southern Central France where a turn eastwards was to be made. This new track took us over the Alps on to the southern side of Lake Maggiore and so far there was no opposition. The aircraft was exactly on estimated time of arrival (ETA) and right on track when we reached Maggiore.

We had climbed to 18,000 feet and began our approach to the mountains. As we passed over in the clear starlit atmosphere it was a sight of utter profundity. Our height was sufficient just to take us clear of the peaks and made easy the identification of Mont Blanc. At such close quarters the whole scene was awe-inspiring.

Maggiore was very well lit and very beautiful in the light of Pathfinder Force flares. At that point we turned south-south-east and began slowly to lose height towards the Italian coast, aiming for a position east of Genoa. On this leg and within a few minutes of the change of course, we sighted an Italian fighter aircraft, an ancient bi-plane – probably a Fiat CR42 – which, at a very prudent distance, fired his single gun. The tracers dropped away well short of us. We replied with the six guns of the rear and upper gun turrets and he left the scene. It was a token attempt, but he had our admiration for his effort – and his wisdom!

Then came the crossing of the sea to La Spezia at a reducing height to near sea level. Preparations for the mine-laying by Roy Evans were completed for the drop of the sea mines. These had to be dropped as low as possible on a line from our island pinpoint at the entry of the bay. We weathered the token attack from the island and made our run over the sea, approaching the sheer cliffs of the Italian mainland.

When it was done we turned round like a snake and began to climb – but trouble came immediately.

The bomb-doors would not close and at once affected our ability to climb back over the Alps. Whilst Andy went aft of the main wing-spar to look into the bomb-bay, Colin and I consulted about the feasibility of flying westward around the Alps and northward through southern and central France. My opinion was that remaining fuel levels made this option doubtful of achievement. However, we were soon relieved: Andy succeeded in closing the bomb doors and the problem evaporated.

So we climbed back to the turning point at Lake Maggiore and flew the reciprocal tracks through France and hit Dungeness on the nose right on ETA. Thereafter as we flew north to base I read out the names of the airfields as the crew called out the morse-code single letter signal lights of each location. It was a relaxing pleasure, rather like being able to read the names of railway stations or pub-signs on a long journey home. It had been a good trip and a long one. Our flying time was 9 hours 10 minutes.

When we had landed and stopped at our dispersal point I rose from my seat to prepare to leave the aircraft. I suddenly realised that I did not have the time to gather up my equipment for I needed to pee more urgently than I had ever done before! I rushed to the back of the aircraft, leapt down the exit ladder and moved smartly to the rear of the aircraft to perform. This took some time and as I moved back to re-enter the aircraft, still doing up my trousers, a group of some four or five people came toward me out of the early morning mist. Just moments before I had uttered: 'By God, I needed that!'

The leading figure in the approaching group was the Air Officer Commanding 5 Group, Bomber Command, Air Marshal Sir Ralph Cochrane, Bt., identifiable the more easily by the load of 'scrambled egg' on the peak his cap. He said: 'Well done, Harris. You must have had a good trip!' and he shook my hand very firmly. The group stood around me for a few moments and then met the rest of the crew as they left the aircraft. His companions were Group Captain 'Sam' Patch (later to become Air Chief Marshal Sir Hubert Patch), together with our CO and our Flight Commander. It was a very pleasurable welcome back. One aircraft had been lost by the Command on the operation.

At that time, my father, who by then had become Lieutenant Bill Harris of the Tatsfield Home Guard (another 'Mainwaring' of the TV series 'Dad's Army'), was invited to visit RAF Biggin Hill, to hear an exact reprise of briefings given to all aircrews in Bomber Command. He was intrigued and impressed by the amount of information we had to digest and of the number of separate sources covering timing, heights to fly, tactics, radio broadcasts during the flight, intelligence concerning defences, meteorological forecasts for the route and over the target area *inter alia*. I asked him if he had been told of the likely behaviour of the gun crews on the island at the head of La Spezia Bay and the comparison of them with our own Home Guard. This had not been a part of his briefing and he was considerably upset at the implied tarnishment of the latter's reputation as worthy soldiers.

Many years later I was told by my friend Hanspeter Osterwalder, the President of the Swiss Avia Oil International Distribution Group of Zurich, that whenever large night-time aircraft groups flew near to or over Swiss territory, elements of the Army were called out and stood to throughout the hours of darkness. He was sympathetic to the Allied cause and always amused by his country's needs when such situations arose. He was an officer in a horse-drawn artillery unit.

About halfway through our time at Skellingthorpe, 4 February to 22 April, the Squadron suffered postings of a number of experienced crews. They remained in 5 Group Bomber Command but came under the command of Wing Commander Guy Gibson as he formed 617, the Dam Buster Squadron. Some experienced leaders like Timber Wood and Trevor-Roper went and a number of complete crews, including one headed by Flight Lieutenant Henry Maudslay, a very popular old-Etonian member of the mess.

We were to meet some of them later at RAF Scampton and to see them more often over the North Sea where most, if not all, night-flying tests or other types of training took place. We noticed that when flying they always wore dark glasses so it was not an unreasonable guess that they were training for a special night job, probably more dangerous than usual – if that was possible at that time!

We were to play a part in one more operation during our service with 50 Squadron. It happened on the night of 20 April. Targets were to be bombed in the Baltic port of Stettin on the northern German coast. We bombed successfully and returned to base on an almost reciprocal track back over the North Sea. The round trip took 7 hours 40 minutes. Thirty-one aircraft were lost and, at this time in 1943, it is appalling to think it was calculated that of every seven aircrew shot down, only one member survived. Accordingly, assuming that all the losses were four-engined aircraft, 31 men might have survived that night, out of a total of 217 missing.

At this point it is, perhaps, appropriate to record that 55,000 aircrew were lost during World War 2 and 25,000 have no known graves.

Immediately after the Stettin trip our crew was posted and from my flying log-book I note that on 5 May we made a routine flight after joining 619 Squadron at Woodhall Spa, reporting to the embryo squadron on 1 May. I do not remember asking my colleagues how they felt, but I did not like quitting 50 Squadron and Skellingthorpe. Certainly we were chosen as an experienced crew to help in the formation of one more squadron – but I would rather have stayed

Ready for action.

where I was. I must attribute the feeling to the leadership at Skellingthorpe, the squadron atmosphere and the good feeling it all produced. The insistence that all aircrew had a daily dose of the sun-ray lamp in the sick quarters was a thoughtful feature of life; you were in trouble if you missed your turn.

We had also become aware that one of the WAAF officers at Skellingthorpe had become attractive to the Wing Commander and he was pressing his case for them to marry. She was resisting because she was already a wartime widow of an RAF flyer. I learned in 1945 that they married after we had left but sadly she lost him, missing on operations. Russell was my idea of a leader, utterly committed to the job: a great man with high standards. We were to miss his quality when we went to Woodhall Spa.

During my service time in Lincolnshire Mary lived in 'digs', first in Lincoln City and then in Woodhall Spa. As often as possible I would join her and one verbal incident of our stay with some good folk in Lincoln lives in our joint memories.

This married couple lived with an aged father and when this senior parent was asked after each supper (when rations permitted) whether he would like some cheese, the response would come with an in-drawing of breath: 'I dursn't, May, I dursn't.'

This worthy phrase has always remained with us!

After leaving 50 Squadron and moving on to Woodhall Spa, Mary and I found accommodation in a comfortable bungalow in the centre of the village; the resident owner, Miss Enderby, was at first reluctant to rent us a room as her previous tenants were a pilot and his wife. When the husband went missing the wife was quite inconsolable and Miss Enderby did not wish to face the possibility of a similar experience. However, we persuaded the good lady to change her mind and she graciously agreed to our moving in. Our present home bears the name 'Woodhall House' – our stay in that village left many memories for Mary and me.

CHAPTER 6

Destruction

'It is your duty to attempt to escape' (Operational briefing)

6 19 Squadron's Commanding Officer was Wing Commander Ian McGhie. Colin and I had met him at Upper Heyford where he was about to start the operational training course. He had not long returned from an overseas posting and was nearing his first taste of the North European bombing offensive. He was short in stature with the well-known RAF officer's trade-mark – a large black moustache. After a re-introduction we saw very little of him during our days at Woodhall Spa. At Heyford he was a well-known customer at the mess bar. He was lost on the famous raid on Peinemunde in September 1943. Every single loss was a tragedy, for all were lively, intelligent, thinking men whose worthiness merited a long and happy life rather than being committed to deal with a vicious and brutal enemy.

We reported to the Officer Commanding 'A' Flight, Squadron Leader Ronnie Churcher, an 'oldster' of twenty-one years of age who much later in his life would be a pilot in the Queen's Flight.

We went to work on the preparation of the aircraft allocated to us, checking everything, including 'swinging' the compass of the aircraft. The latter was a ticklish business involving the establishment of the deviation of that instrument. Compass deviation is the amount by which the compass needle is affected by the metals present in the aircraft and is corrected by delicate changes to compensating magnets in the base of the compass itself.

Forty hours of flying, including training, took place before the day of the first operational flight of the whole squadron. We had already lost one aircraft and crew which had taken off one day for a test flight over the North Sea and never returned.

The squadron's first operational flight was targeted on Düsseldorf on 11/12 June 1943 – the Whitsun weekend. It was to be a high level bombing mission to be executed at 22,000 feet.

The weather was fine with no moon and we left the English coast at our planned cruising height at 0013 hours. It had been an exceptional take-off for each aircraft carried, for the first time, the heaviest bomb-load ever. With such a large all-up aircraft weight it would be necessary to take the engine throttle levers 'through the gate' for maximum power at 14 lbs. of fuel-boost. In all our previous flying, offensive or otherwise, it had been stressed that the throttles were not to be positioned beyond a certain obvious stop – the gate. This ensured that 8 lbs. only of fuel-boost was delivered to the engines. To go beyond it would have added another unknown engine stress factor for take-off but the need for extra boost was certainly required on the night of 11 June.

I thought we would never stop bouncing as the end of the runway approached. Every yard of concrete was needed and the rate of climb to the eastern seaboard was noticeably slower than usual. We set course from a point over Mablethorpe where the shore was well-defined and made for the enemy coast. As the navigator I had no reason other than to assume that the flight was proceeding as usual save for the inevitable and oncoming target inhospitality; however, about halfway across the sea to the Frisian islands at the enemy coast, that assumption proved not to be valid.

The air-speed indicators in the pilot's and my own instrument panels failed suddenly, showing a ridiculously low air speed. We were not flying in icing conditions nor could we think of any other likely reason, especially as the indicators had earlier behaved normally at take-off and thereafter. This instrument is vital: in order to navigate accurately one must know the indicated air speed (IAS) and the pilot must also know this speed in order to be able to manoeuvre the aircraft. It is particularly important in the maintenance of a constant 'corkscrewing' through the air to confuse anti-aircraft gunners and to fly the aircraft to its fullest performance ability during an enemy night-fighter attack. Operationally the instrument failure was a disaster.

Colin Taylor spoke to us all in turn, seeking our opinion as to whether we should go on to the target or abort the flight. My own reply, so far as I can remember, was that such a final decision was for him, the captain, but for the reasons I have already stated here, I said that the odds were stacked heavily against a successful mission. Navigational accuracy and reasonable aircraft performance had already been lost. The increased all-up weight and the loss of the

SA

HEAVIEST BOMB LOAD

DUSSELDORF THE MAIN TARGET: "A VERY HEAVY ATTACK"

200 Fortresses Pound North German Ports

A.F. Bomber Command during the night broke a lull lasting 12 days by making the greatest attack on many since the war began. Dusseldorf, the great inland on the Rhine, was the main target.

The number of bombers engaged in the raid was the biggest since the 1,000-plane raids last year. The tonnage of bombs dropped was the heaviest so far.

The attack made on Dusseldorf itself is officially described as "very heavy."

The raid followed a mass attack by 200 American Flying Fortresses on the North German U-boat bases of Wilhelmshaven and Cuxhaven, in one of the greatest day raids so far of the war.

The night attack on Dusseldorf ended the longest after-dark bombing lull on Germany this year. It was the 13th night after the great raid on Wuppertal on May 29.

Admitting a raid on "Western Germany," Berlin radio to-day asserted that 96 British bombers were shot down.

It was Dusseldorf's second heavy battering within less than three weeks. The last raid, on the night of May 25, was made by a force not far short of 1,000 bombers, and nearly 2,000 tons of bombs were dropped.

Dusseldorf (population 450,000), on the Rhine, 24 miles north-west of Cologne is Germany's third largest inland port. The most important target is the Rheinmetall undertaking, the second largest steel works in Germany. Fifty thousand people work in its two vast plants in the eastern outskirts of the city.

Altogether the city has been raided 53 times.

HOUR ATTACK ON DUSSELDORF

"GREAT DAMAGE": 43 BOMBERS MISSING

Air Ministry communique: Aircraft of Bomber Command were over Germany in very great strength last night. Dusseldorf was the main objective and a highly concentrated attack was delivered in just over an hour. Preliminary reports indicate that great damage was done.

A smaller force attacked Munster, where good results were achieved. Several other targets in Ruhr and Rhineland were bombed. From these operations 43 of our bombers are missing.

An enemy aircraft was destroyed by one of our fighters on intruder patrol.

RECORD NUMBER OF HEAVY BOMBERS

The number of heavy bombers dispatched last night was the greatest yet engaged on any night. The ground defences at Dusseldorf were strong at the beginning, but were saturated by the weight of the attack.

ON GERMANY YET

62

airspeed indicator were serious adverse factors reducing aircraft manoeuvrability. After Colin had taken the views of all of us, he decided that we should go on. It was militarily the right decision to take.

The electronic navigational instrument 'Gee', so accurate over the UK, was already beginning to be affected by German jamming. In our pre-flight briefing we had been told that a technical addition had been made to the circuitry of 'Gee' with the direct aim of reducing the effect of enemy interference. Early evidence on the screen as we approached the enemy coast seemed to suggest to me that the modification was ineffective but it was always possible that its usefulness might be extended a little further than usual into Occupied European airspace: one had to wait and see. No comment came from Roy Evans in the nose of the aircraft as to the accuracy of our crossing point at the enemy coastline which suggested to me that our loss of the airspeed indicator had not, so far, caused a drift from our intended track. We proceeded on course and, in due time, penetrated German airspace. From the last near-reasonable reading on 'Gee' before jamming blotted out the signals, I calculated that we were drifting slightly south of track, not seriously but enough to warrant a small change to our compass heading. I gave the new course to Colin.

Almost immediately thereafter we were attacked from a lower level astern. There were sharp warning cries from Ronnie Chisholm and Billy Henderson, the rear and mid-upper gunners. We turned sluggishly to port. The intercom system from both air-gunner positions remained switched on. Gunfire sounded loud and clear. I waited for the effect of fire from the enemy fighter. He had come in from below on the port quarter raking the aircraft with his cannon fire. He came round for a second attack and hung on our tail momentarily too long. One heard the chatter of Ronnie's guns. There was a sudden cry from each of the gunners: 'He's gone – he's blown up!'

But we were mortally crippled.

Colin brought us back slowly onto our original heading and checked that all on board were safe and uninjured.

Stock was taken of our damage situation. Three engines were on fire, the hydraulically controlled variable pitch mechanism on all four propellers had been damaged and all had gone into fine pitch and very high revolutions per minute (rpm). They had lost their bite into the air and propulsion of the aircraft was zero. The more we tried to maintain height the higher the engine revolutions mounted with an deafening and whining roar. The effect on airspeed and attempts to maintain height continued to be ineffective. Heavy damage had been inflicted on wings, ailerons and fuselage. The tailplane and the twin tail fins had been badly damaged. Colin was in acute difficulty trying to keep the aircraft straight and level – or even in the air. The rear-gunner's armour plating between the two pairs of Browning machine guns had been pierced by a cannon shell. Ronnie Chisholm reported that the shell must have passed between his legs but he was unhurt.

'A good job it wasn't a little bit higher, Ronnie,' said an unremembered voice laconically. A sense of humour prevailed!

The decision was taken to jettison the bomb-load. Clearly the hydraulics still worked for the bomb doors opened and shut. As soon as the bombs were away – to fall on enemy territory – we gingerly turned 180 degrees with a view to returning to base. It seemed to me to be rather like a newspaper boy throwing the papers on the step rather than putting them through the letter-box.

Fires in two engines had been extinguished leaving the third, the starboard outer, to continue to flare. The Lancaster continued to lose height at a serious rate and flew on in this manner for another fifteen minutes when we took stock of our position again.

The starboard outer fire was becoming more intense and Cecil Anderson felt that it was possible that the lubricant header tank in that engine nacelle might be burning out and perhaps we should wait just a short time for this to take place. The crew was aware that gasoline vapour in the ullage (empty space) in the wing fuel tanks was now a very pregnant explosive danger which increased as the fire in the engine persisted. It was a basic case of bale out or get blown out in pieces.

The order was given: 'Abandon aircraft, abandon, abandon!' Our height was near 13,000 feet when we quit the Lancaster.

I put on my chest parachute, threw all the contents of my pockets onto the navigation table and followed Roy Evans and Cecil Anderson out of the forward hatch in the nose of the aircraft. Douglas Inggs left his seat at the radio to follow me. Colin Taylor was the last to leave, and had some difficulty because as he attempted to leave his seat and ceased to operate the flying controls the aircraft fell away immediately. Ronnie Chisholm and Billy Henderson had departed by falling out of the rear turret and from the rear fuselage door respectively.

I had squatted momentarily on the edge of the roaring black hole which was the escape hatch and rolled out. I do not remember pulling the cord on the chute and was temporarily knocked senseless. When I came round the aircraft was still within hearing distance but in just a few moments it was gone and all was perfectly and eerily quiet. I had been hit by the 'chute' harness and my face was well bloodied; the descent took several minutes. At the beginning of the fall I felt sure that there was a light shining on my face – had I arrived in Heaven complete with halo? I eventually worked out that a large torch which I had stuffed into my battledress had switched itself on and was shining into my eyes!

I hit the ground very firmly and fell back on my bottom.

My immediate reaction was to pull the parachute into a pile before me. I had landed in the middle of a wheat field on a clear starlit night at about 0145 hours. Everything was so still. I remained motionless for some ten minutes or so, then rolled up the parachute more tightly and left it where I had fallen. I figured that the crop would not be cut for a while and the 'chute would remain hidden for a time. I crawled out of the field down onto a narrow unmade road and sat on the bank. If I was to attempt an escape I had to get going quickly. The advice we had been given was to get away from the scene. I unpacked my escape kit, a shallow perspex box. It held a silk scarf with a Low Countries map printed thereon, French, Dutch and Belgian bank notes, benzadrine and Horlicks tablets, chewing gum and a very small compass the size of a trouser button. I distributed the items about my person, ditched my large aircrew torch and promptly lost the compass in the long grass – a marvellous start. I was clearly not in the Dick Barton league (1943 vintage special agent) nor of the James Bond ilk in the 1970s. It was clearly not my day.

So with my back to Polaris, the North Star, I took off down the track. I had not gone far when I heard the high-pitched bellow of a cow in pain. I doubled my speed and soon reached a narrow metalled road. The signpost close by indicated that the village of Tongres was but twelve kilometres northwards. At this point about forty minutes had passed since bale-out. I was in Belgium, probably some 15-20 miles north of the city of Liège.

Years later I learned from Colin Taylor that when he reached the ground, after baling out, he landed on the back of a cow! Was this the bellow of alarm that I heard? Had I missed an opportunity to join up with Colin? – he had eventually made an escape through Belgium, France and Spain to Gibraltar and home. Had I made too much haste at that time? – we shall never know.

I decided that I would stay on the road until daybreak as long as it ran southwards. I would begin cross-country running when it was light or if the circumstances demanded. My long distance aim was to pass through Belgium and thence to the south of France and then on to the Pyrenees, into Spain and finally into Gibraltar. I remember the quiet, sleeping hamlets and the long straight road. At the first sign of light I saw my first Belgian worker on a bicycle. He passed me without a sound. I pressed on and began to see one or two more worker cyclists. Eventually, on a bend in the road I stopped momentarily to consider whether it was time to begin crossing the open countryside. At that point one of the early morning cyclists stopped and uttered: *'Bonjour, monsieur.'*

I spoke French understandably but not up to present-day 'A' level. When he said: *'Venez avec moi'* (Come with me), I followed and was ready to say: *'Je suis aviateur anglais, pourriez-vous m'aider?'* (I am an English airman. Could you help me?) In my uniform it was quite obvious but the question did arise many times later that first day.

My new friend led me off the road to an orchard and into a small milking shed and invited me to rest there.

Three or four people were seated at the rear end of cows and a drink of warm milk was quickly produced for me. We talked a little but after thirty minutes or so they asked me to leave. I moved out after two hard-boiled eggs and some strawberries were given to me. I ate them later in the morning but have never since mixed the two items!

By this time it was full daylight and I began to run south across the fields and lanes. The intervals of time between incidents is not now clear to me, but I can recall the order in which they happened. I had come upon a small village and was running behind a row of cottages when a man came out of his back-door, saw me coming and shouted:

'Attendez, monsieur!' (Wait a moment.)

We talked a little over the rear garden fence and he asked me the direction I was taking. I replied: *'Vers le sud.'* (Southwards.)

It amused him and I understood him to say: '*En ces vêtements?*
Comment? C'est incroyable!' (In those clothes! How? It's unbelievable!')

So saying, he immediately took off his jacket and insisted that I put
it on over my battledress. He very conveniently had a safety pin in
his pocket and with it secured the lapels under my chin. That done
he wished me well and gave me a Belgian banknote which, at the
time, had a value of £5. We shook hands warmly and I was on my
way. '*Allez-vous en,*' he said. (Get out of here!)

I was in disguise and soon thereafter I made two attempts to get
help.

Moving across the landscape of Belgium, just like anywhere else for
that matter, there are an infinite number of obstacles which have
strong effects on one's efforts to keep a constant heading. In so doing
I passed round or through small hamlets, some of which had a
church. I quietly entered two of these and in each case found the
priest at early morning personal prayer. Each time I waited in a pew at
the western end of the church until they arose from the altar rail.
They each gave me a similar response. 'I am sorry I cannot assist. I
have a duty to my congregation which, in these very bad times, has a
need for my presence. A great deal would be lost by my flock if I
became occupied in helping you or your colleagues. I would ask you
please to move on immediately.'

Breaking through onto another road I met a man walking his dog.
In spite of my 'disguise' he immediately identified me and invited
me to walk back to his home to take coffee. He was a teacher and we
sat together and sipped our coffee at the front room window. I saw
my first German go by, driving a military horse and cart full of hay
and moving very slowly. It was almost beyond acceptance that he
was the enemy and I was observing such an event. Twelve hours
before I was still amongst my own countrymen. But time pressed a
little and my friend said I should move on. He produced two bicycles
and instructed me to ride fifty metres behind him until we reached a
main road which would run south for many kilometres. We had
gone barely two hundred metres when my front tyre was punctured.
My friend walked back and looked fiercely at my machine. He was
very distressed and exclaimed that the failure of the bike was too
much for him to bear. '*C'est trop ça, monsieur. Je dois partir
immédiatement!*' (It's too much! I must leave right away!) In a few
moments he had gone.

I elected to begin to cross the countryside directly again, the better to maintain my southerly route. I moved at a run across an open field from which cabbages had been recently harvested. I had gone no further than fifty metres when I heard a loud shout – *'Attendez!'* (Wait!)

A Belgian gendarme had left his bicycle in the road and was striding towards me. For a moment an intelligence briefing about such men came to mind: if they were wearing leather gaiters they were reliable and co-operative. If they were wearing German-style jackboots, avoid them. I took an almost immediate decision to continue running, reasoning that if my information was reliable he would not attempt to stop me. I was absolutely wrong. The next sound I heard was a very loud voice saying: *'Arrêtez-vous!'* ('Stop!')

I stopped and turned to face him. He came forward with his revolver drawn but as he moved he returned it to its holster and said in French: 'You are an airman?'

Replying in French I said I thought it was obvious. He said that it was indeed.

We shook hands and I showed him my uniform with flying badges under my disguise. (By this time I was feeling some discomfort wearing two jackets in mild weather). We squatted down in the field and talked a little. When we rose to part he asked me which way I intended to go. I pointed a finger southwards, but he called me an idiot and said that I should change my mind and direction; if I did this I would outflank German search patrols which were coming towards us across the countryside. We were standing in typical Belgian open country and clearly I should get going. We shook hands again. This was the only time that a man with a revolver would give me a handshake and a smile.

I did as I was bidden and ran hard in the new direction. It was hard going because buildings, minor roads and natural obstacles tiresomely persisted in diverting me, but my battledress was drying well. In the early periods of cross-country travel I had become soaked with heavy dew and it had made the blue serge very heavy.

At about midday, to the best of my recollection, I approached a more important road for two-way traffic. A hundred metres away to the north I saw a two-wheeled cart drawn by a horse with a short figure of a man walking at its head. I waited for him to reach me.

'Bonjour monsieur. Je suis aviateur anglais. Est-ce que je peux vous

accompagner?' (Good day, sir. I am an English airman. May I walk along with you?)

He replied affirmatively but it was difficult to understand his French for he had a cleft palate. His attitude was clearly friendly and we walked together for some time. He said he had to go near to Liège and it would take some time but I was welcome to stay with him. As the conversation continued he said he would leave me at a house where he was sure I would be given help. We moved slowly across the flat country along a road bordered here and there by poplars.

Suddenly he said: *'Regardez en avant à deux cent metres, mon vieux.'* (Look ahead two hundred metres, my friend.)

I could see a road-block some distance ahead which was manned by one gendarme. We stopped and had a few words about tactics; my friend said that I was to lead the horse, smoke one of his cigarettes and all would be well. He rolled me one of his own specials, giving it a good lick and a flourish. For a non-smoker it was dreadful but complementary to my 'disguise'!

I took the horse's bridle and we began our approach. However, within fifty metres or so my new-found friend began to shout things at me which I only partly understood. I stopped the horse and went to the rear of the cart and said: *'Qu'est ce qui se passe?'* (What's happening?)

'Vous vous êtes enmerdés et vous êtes idiot!' (You are an absolute shit and a total idiot!)

I got the drift – I was leading the horse toward the left-hand side of the road and as far as my friend was concerned I was an absolute fool. He was right and I went back to the horse and started again. I had to exercise some care with the horse and cart as we went through the awkwardly placed barriers. The gendarme, the sole guardian, paid no attention to us – and he wore German issue jackboots!

We were through in moments which seemed longer than usual – very much longer – and walked on until the carter came forward and said that I must be tired and invited me to get up into the near empty cart and lie down out of sight. He said he would wake me when we reached the house where he intended to leave me and after some time we stopped at the dropping point. It had been very good to lie down.

My refuge was not a house at all but a corrugated iron affair which was gradually collapsing. The deterioration had gone so far that in order to enter I had to duck down sideways to the right to get inside.

The doorway was some 40 degrees out of the vertical. Within were three individuals, husband, wife and son of about eleven or twelve years of age. In a scene of abject poverty, father and son were both lying ill, the boy obviously very much worse than his father. Each lay on separate piles of filthy rags and old blankets. The woman was on her feet, looking pale and very tired but clearly not affected by the illness. They had no food and no water in the building and neither money nor medication. My carter friend talked with her a little and she agreed to allow me to remain a while. He then left and we began to talk. She said I could not possibly stay with them but she would be glad to take me in to Liège if that would help. I readily agreed and told her I should be pleased if she could lead me to the central railway station where I would, hopefully, catch a train for Brussels. A simple plan was agreed: I was to follow her to an out-of-city tram terminus whence we would take a ride directly to the station. After buying the ticket she would ride in the front carriage and I would stand on the rear platform. She explained the plan to her husband and son. The point was reached when goodbyes had to be said. I shook hands with the father, an Englishman and a veteran of World War 1. I turned to the boy who was appallingly ill and of a grey-yellow colour. He asked if I would kiss him before I went and for a few moments I did not know quite what to do; my fear was that he was dying of tuberculosis. I did the next best thing and put my cheek against his forehead and held it there for a second or two. He seemed pleased and we left shortly thereafter. I handed the woman the Belgian banknote given to me earlier in the day.

It was a longish walk to the terminus during which I followed at a distance of about seventy-five metres. We boarded a tram; she paid the fare and we took our agreed positions. It was a bizarre thirty minute journey which became busier as we moved in toward the centre of the city. Belgian people and German soldiers, either with shopping or rifles, climbed on or alighted and in so doing shaped an extraordinary scene for me. It was utterly ridiculous that an escaping airman with a flimsy disguise and who left enemy territory just a little over twelve hours before, could be in such a situation.

I met a friendly stranger on the tram platform who stood opposite me and who pointed unobtrusively to my midriff and said quietly: 'La montre, monsieur.' (The watch, Sir.)

He had directed my attention to the Air Ministry navigation watch which I was showing as I stood with arms folded across my chest. I thanked him and quickly removed the offending item. He was the third Belgian to penetrate the 'disguise'.

After a tense half-hour we finally reached the main railway station. My guide bought a ticket for Brussels for me and we parted, me with my ticket and she with all my Belgian and Dutch cash – in sterling terms probably £10. I figured that I was in enough trouble and £10 worth of Belgian francs and Dutch guilders was not likely to make a great deal of difference to my future – but it might help her and her sick family a good deal more.

I moved towards the platforms and asked a railwayman: 'Bruxelles direct?' (Brussels express?). The appropriate platform number was given and I waited on the edge of a group of expectant travellers and after twenty minutes or so the train appeared. It moved slowly along the platform and those waiting moved forward. One lady was over-eager and moved too far too quickly and succeeded in falling down between the moving carriages and the low platform. Screams erupted and a fair degree of agitation followed. I moved away slowly and boarded the train near the engine – quite alone.

Once aboard I discovered the train to be jam-packed with people. The journey was to be a standing one and I wondered how long the train might take. From Liège to Brussels would, I estimated, take one and a half hours and at the end of the period I should recognise the station by its size. It was hot and my disguise held. Nothing seemed out of the ordinary as we moved along. I was unaware at the time but discovered later that every express (direct) train carried a German patrol of two or three men, checking that all passengers had their papers or travel permits. The incident of the lady falling off the platform had made me move well forward and the patrol must have been moving slowly in my direction, but failed to reach my position on the train. I thought about it later and was grateful to the poor woman.

I remained alert and one hour and twenty minutes later the train stopped at a most impressive station; my immediate reaction was that we had made the journey in good time and I was in Brussels, but I could not have been much more adrift. I was the first one off the train and through the ticket barrier. The ticket collector said something to me but I was not stopping for anyone and quit the station very speedily. When I got well outside the building it was very clear that I had descended at the wrong station. This was Louvain and I had burned one of my boats – perhaps all of them – and I knew then what the railwayman must have been trying to tell me!

What was I to do now other than walk further into town and try my luck? This I did and came to a park where I was able to sit and rest unnoticed. The whole area was alive with students walking, talking and studying, seated on park benches or on the grass. They were, of course, from the University. I started walking again and then saw a young priest approaching me. I stopped him and told him who I was and asked if he could help me. At once he became agitated and exclaimed quickly: '*Non, non monsieur, je ne travaille pas pour l'état.*' (No, no, sir, I do not work for the state – at least that is what I thought he said.) He ran away from me and disappeared very quickly.

The time had now reached 1730 hours and I knew it was imperative to have a plan of some sort, which swiftly formed in my mind. I would throw all caution to the winds, move around the town a little more and take a chance somewhere – as if I had not taken plenty already! This opportunity came a little later in the old quarter of Louvain where I saw a very large fellow standing in the doorway of a very small shop. The two windows each had a picture for sale and it seemed to me that he might have plenty of time to listen to me. I approached, told him my story and waited for an answer. It came quickly: '*Entrez, monsieur. Asseyez-vous ici.*' (Come in, Sir. Sit down here.)

I sat where he bade me in a room just behind the shop. He said he would leave me and return with help in a short time. He did so and was accompanied by a second man with a bicycle. I was to follow him at fifty metres distance and would soon be in friendly hands.

We came to a large double-fronted house high above the footpath; I followed my guide up the steps and was taken into a large sitting room. I talked with two men about my landing some sixteen hours before and defined the point south of Tongres. They were surprised I had come so far in such a short time. Finally, they said they would help me but I should be prepared to answer many more questions in order to prove my bona fides. So saying, I was taken by the original messenger to a house in the old quarter of Louvain. Thus ended my first day on the run. I knew I was alive and well but no one back home would hear of my fate for nearly six months.

CHAPTER 7

Evasion

The house where I had arrived was old and admitted little daylight; the ceilings were low and the rooms very small. It was occupied by a woman and her son. There began a very awkward period with my new companions: I was profoundly grateful for the hiding place, but the son made life very difficult. He was possibly thirty years old and mentally defective; he harassed me most of the day even to the point of eyeing me through a knot-hole in the lavatory door – a seat-with-bucket job.

After seven days I was visited by an English lady who questioned me very closely about my family background and my knowledge of the part of the south-east of England in which Tatsfield was to be found and of London, where I had spent my early working days.

Q: What does your father do?

A: He is a postmaster and has a general store.

Q: What part does your mother play?

A: She supports my father in every way. She is not a well person.

Q: Do you have a garden? Describe what is in it.

A: It is about a quarter of an acre, has a lawn with fruit trees and a large vegetable plot.

Q: Does your mother do the gardening, are there any flowers?

A: No and there are just a few flowers.

Q: You tell me you worked in London for a while. You must have some knowledge of the Underground. What is the next station going west from Victoria on the Circle Line?

A: (Pause for considerable thought) Sloane Square.

She told me that the information I had given would be radioed to London for verification and I could expect her return in four or five days. I have often wondered whether anything dire would have happened to me had I not answered 'Sloane Square'.

I must now digress and briefly return to Tatsfield. In 1943 the population of the village was probably around 800. Not all those people were customers of my father but as postmaster he was known by everyone. The head of one of the families with whom he had little to do, knew more about me than my parents or my wife did at that time. This knowledge ran almost from the moment we failed to return, when I was posted 'missing in operations against the enemy'. This particular Tatsfield resident was a Civil Servant at the Foreign Office and head of the section which handled radio messages to and from underground organisations in Occupied Europe. From the radio messages received he knew that I was alive but could do nothing to help my wife's and my parents' anxieties.

After some time, however, his wife made a point of coming to see my mother whom she addressed more or less as follows: 'Mrs Harris, we do not know each other very well but I am, of course, aware that your son is missing. It may help you when I tell you that last night I had a very vivid dream in which I met your son who was very much alive. I just had to come in and tell you about it.'

When the war was at an end my parents were told the full story.

I now return to my narrative.

In about a week my interrogator returned to tell me that she had been told that a radio message from London had cleared me as genuine. She explained that this clearance procedure was now an essential part of their drill as there had been a number of dangerous and damaging infiltrations of the escape system by enemy agents. The infiltrations were very recent and I could expect my progress to be slow as a result. I accepted the position but appealed to her to get me away from my present hiding place if she could. I explained how much trouble I was getting from the widow's son. She promised to try to do something to help and on this particular occasion gave me a suit to wear and took away my uniform to be burned.

I can remember this period pretty well but am uncertain as to the order of events and the amount of time that passed between and during each of the hiding places. Nor am I completely confident that I remember every concealment, but I believe they moved me on from the widow four or five days after my request. I think she and her son took money for my stay and there might have been a commitment on both sides to keep me there longer than was the case. These two people were very poor; there was little food or furniture, almost no lighting and very primitive facilities overall. It was a great relief to be going to alternative shelter and I was grateful to be moving on. I learned that movement between hiding-places generally took place near to curfew time at 2230 hours as at that time of day suspicion was not aroused by people moving around quickly. The fear of transgressing the law was great and it would be assumed that running figures were obediently hastening to their various destinations within the time prescribed.

From the widow's house I was taken from place to place by a young man, a good English speaker, usually just before curfew. My next hole-up was in a small apartment over a bar. Here I was made welcome but the greeting was tempered, as it was almost always, with an apology that there was very little food for me. An alternative was offered in that I could drink as much beer as I liked! I did not take advantage in this regard but certainly I drank more beer than usual. The bar room was long and narrow with a urinal at the rear and I descended a very old cast-iron spiral staircase to relieve myself during the day. The frequency of my visits was enhanced by the intake of beer – Stella Artois, the very one! After a few days we decided that beer drinking should be curtailed for the risk of my being discovered in the lavatory was too great, the clientele of the bar being mainly German soldiers.

There was indeed no food; at this establishment I had a daily ration of blueberries with just a few potatoes every fourth or fifth day. I slept on a couch in the room immediately above the bar whilst the bar-keeper, his wife and ancient father-in-law occupied the rooms on the second and third floors. The old man rose late in the morning and staggered down passing through my quarters with a large well-filled pot held in a shaking hand, *en route* down the spiral staircase to the lavatory. Life was a bit tense at those moments of ancient toiletry and, indeed, I lived for twelve hours each day above the loud voices of the German customers.

The young courier who had replaced my English lady interrogator had, within a few days, taken me to the next link in the chain. It may have been on this occasion that the change was made at around midday. My English-speaking guide was keen to show me the central parts of Louvain and during this walk we were caught up in a throng of uniformed German railway officials who were just coming out of a building *en masse*, all complete with side-arms. My friend continued to speak English, despite my quiet remonstrations, assuring me that 'They'll never notice us here.'

I was not much pacified for, having recently been almost destroyed by gunfire, I had developed an over-weening respect for armed Germans and recognised early in our acquaintanceship that this young man, his bulging document case always at the ready, was too boastful and arrogant for my liking – but he was risking his life to help me and I was grateful. However, as long as I was in his care I wished he would cut down on unnecessary risk-taking in both our interests.

My next lodging was a small street-corner house occupied by a man, his common-law wife and a young child, a pretty girl of about eight or nine years of age. I slept in the small downstairs sitting-room and during the day had a good view of the trafficked road which ran by. The family needed cash and they were paid for my lodging by my guide. The man of the house had no work and I was to discover the reason after several conversations with him: he had not long come out of prison where he had served a term for embezzlement of the funds of his employer, a lawyer. He told me that he was a very worried man because neither his erstwhile employer nor the police had discovered all the rascally things he had been up to and he feared the consequences any time there was a knock at the door. This had a bearing on me for my guide had instructed me to move quickly to the rear of the dwelling if there was sharp knocking on the front door. A difficulty arose when this actually happened for both my host and I were moving shoulder to shoulder in the passageway to the back door – he being fearful that he had been found out again and I wondering whether my arrest by the Gestapo was imminent. I can remember that scene and smile about our haste, but it was not amusing at the time!

There were two or three more safe houses to come and all involved short stays. Visits to a photographer took place where passport size pictures for a Belgian identity card were taken. I spent some time with the photographer during which he showed me his files of negatives and photographic prints of German/civil functions and other events which had taken place since the beginning of the Occupation in 1940. These pictures he intended to use as evidence of Belgian collaboration with the enemy and this would be sufficient to serve to support an eventual indictment. The case was all there in pictures but I learned after the war that he had been shot when an escaping airman was found hiding on his premises.

Trips were made to collect a different suit, shirt and tie. We made a call also to collect my identity card. The photograph was properly attached, my signature was required and I discovered that I had been born in Schaarbeek just outside Brussels. There were two accuracies on the card; my picture and my date of birth. Heaven knows which office and which person did the issuing of the card; I was certainly one of their satisfied customers!

One of the most comfortable hiding places, yet at one juncture, one of the most charged with atmosphere and difficulty, was the home of a family of five – father, mother and three teenage children, two daughters and a son. I had a room to myself with a comfortable bed and all the facilities one needs. My stay there almost certainly stretched to two weeks and I was made to feel as relaxed as possible. Halfway through my stay I became ill. We all diagnosed the problem as a severe attack of asthma, but how could we deal with it? There was considerable discussion round the large table in the kitchen. Mother and father were of the opinion that it was caused by stress. It was too dangerous to call a doctor; that idea was instantly dismissed. One of the family recalled that Cousin Albert had experienced a similar condition. One of the daughters was despatched to bring in Albert and, within the hour, he was with us.

'*Oui, bien sûr, c'est l'asthme.*' said he. (Yes, certainly it's asthma.)

'*Qu'est ce qu'on peut faire?*' (What can be done?)

Poor Albert certainly must have been taken aback, having to deal unexpectedly and on the spot with an affair of great personal risk.

'*J'ai des choses à la maison, je crois.*' (I have some things at home, I believe.)

'*Allez-vous en.*' (Get going!) was the advice he got. He went and was back again shortly to take from his pocket four or five ampoules of a liquid and a tin box (so old that all the paint had been worn off) in which was a hypodermic syringe.

A short and sharp debate followed as to who was going to treat the patient. At the end of the discussion it was decided unanimously that I was the best person to make the injection. There was nothing I could do but accept the job. I remembered my mother saying that it was necessary to boil such things as hypodermics for twenty minutes before they could be considered sterile. This was done and I withdrew the contents of one of the ampoules into the syringe. I remembered the need to expel all the air from the needle and into my arm it went. I was despatched to bed and slept for fourteen hours without stirring!

Members of the family took turns, hour by hour, to keep watch in my room. Everyone breathed more easily when I woke up – including me! I was much better; we had not had much choice but thankfully it had worked.

I enjoyed talking with this family each of whom found the occupation of their country the worst kind of existence. The son was especially active in underground activities and often carried a handgun. One day, as we talked, he plunged his hand into the inside pocket of his jacket and extracted a revolver. It was a giant job – in retrospect the sort of weapon only Clint Eastwood would carry around in spaghetti Western movies!

During my stay with this family there began to be talk from my courier that there was an early prospect of moving on and out of Louvain. Departure was not definite but the destination was likely to be Brussels. It was a case of wait and see – of which commodity there had already been a generous supply. This edge-of-the-seat stuff, by this time, was stretching my nerves more than a little.

Action did follow quickly and a move to an apartment in the centre of Louvain was made for two nights, in readiness for the journey. I was to travel by long-distance tram under the guidance of another lady member of the organisation. The ticket would be bought for me and I was to travel in the rear carriage of the tram. The journey would take some time and I was alerted to the probability that there would be a point between the two cities where the tram would be stopped and boarded by the occupying forces. Ostensibly this halt was to check identity papers but, more importantly for the local German forces, it was an opportunity to confiscate all vegetables carried by passengers; this activity had become routine. Many housewives from the capital were going out into the country to buy vegetables which were not available in the shops, so the ladies went to the sources of supply. The Germans also were short of vegetables so confiscation of travellers' shopping was a part-answer to their problem. I was worried about this prospect of confrontation. I was also briefed on the transfer procedure from one guide to another when in Brussels: my lady guide and I were to enter a large church, kneel down and await the arrival of a third person, a woman, who would kneel on my left. When she rose to leave I was to follow her without hesitation.

The departure day came at last and the journey began. At about the halfway point the tram was stopped and a small group of German military approached; some guarded the boarding points while the remainder, three soldiers, came slowly through the two carriages. Their entry into my carriage meant that my guide was safe and as they came nearer to me my pulse rate climbed very steeply. All to no purpose, for the examination of my brand new identity card was perfunctory and we resumed the journey. I relaxed just a little and my pulse dropped from 130 to 125. The invaders had made a modest haul of green vegetables and I wondered if the officers' mess would get its share that evening – would the distribution be equitable? A pointless thought.

In the centre of Brussels we made our way into a very large church up a broad flight of steps and through the main west door. We knelt in a pew in the centre of the nave and were joined quite soon by a lady in her mid-sixties. She rose eventually and I followed a short distance behind; when we were outside a second lady came forward whom I followed. I had been told that at this point I was to look out for a very tall man in a white raincoat. There he was! Again I followed discreetly.

We boarded a jam-packed tram going out of the city – a journey of twenty minutes plus, along the borders of a rich residential area. A short walk from the tram stop took us to a five-barred gate in the centre of a fifty metre frontage of a beautiful house.

'Donhead' was built in a chalet-like style with very deep overhanging eaves along the front of the building and over the entrance where we were greeted by the chatelaine. The main salon was large and beautifully furnished with a full-size grand piano near one of the windows. We sat together in the centre of the room while the courier and Madame conversed in French about the arrangements connected with my stay. My guide soon departed and I was immediately given a tour of the house by Madame Ninette Jeanty. All the rooms were furnished with taste, style and quality. In my hostess' studio there was a large banner along one wall which almost shouted (in English) 'ARE WE DOWNHEARTED? – NO!' I was shown the false back to an upstairs cupboard quite near to the bedroom I was to occupy. It was the entrance to those deep eaves and the roof-space over the main door. This was to be my hiding-place if there should be any problem, but such an eventuality was considered to be unlikely.

The tour over, we awaited the return home of Mme. Jeanty's husband Paul and son Claude aged fifteen years. My stay of seven days or thereabouts had begun. Ninette Jeanty was a lively, intelligent, authoritative and confident woman, a blonde of medium height who had a purposeful stride. She spoke English fluently with a very marked but attractive French accent; she was indeed a charming person for whom one had immediate respect.

Claude was the first to return but Paul, the husband, a practising advocate in the High Court, came much later. By that time I had been directed to my room, it having been decided by Mme Jeanty that I should be out of sight as much as possible.

We talked together each evening when I found Paul Jeanty to be an extremely likeable and patient man. When we first met he had insisted that I narrate, in French, the story of my evasion since baling out. Ninette Jeanty would play the piano now and then during the day-time and always during each evening. It was August and we were able to spend time in the garden, taking care not to be seen from the gateway or the road. I was able to do two or three pencilled drawings of the house and garden.

There were many books in my room, a few in English (all novels by Charles Morgan), the rest in French. I struggled with *The Fountain* and *Sparkenbroke* but made little headway. I remember how Morgan treats his characters, particularly when they are falling in love. It took three pages of unparagraphed prose to discuss falling in, recognising, becoming fully aware of, the psychological problem of being in, confessing and applying love! Perhaps this is why his books have more appeal in continental Europe than in England although I have no valid reason for suggesting it. I had been married for a little under a year and had none of the problems that Morgan's lovers had, but it passed some time! Perhaps I was an ignorant philistine, but I look back now and take the view that he, Charles Morgan, must have been a gentle, thoughtful fellow. I have since discovered that he served in the Royal Navy during World War 2 – that would excuse more or less anything.

After I had been with the Jeantys for five or six days there came a message that I might be moving fairly soon. It was likely that I would be taken into the country to a landing strip and flown home. This news, if it turned out to be true, would mean a Westland Lysander aircraft; I was greatly encouraged. A strong element of hope that I might actually get back surged up within me and I slept a little better, but that hope was short-lived.

At 4.30 am one morning, two or three days later, I was awakened by Ninette Jeanty.

'The Germans are at the door. Into the cupboard quickly. I shall get into your bed.'

The partition closed behind me and I crawled in complete darkness away from my point of entry into the roof-space. I had no clothes on save for a pair of underpants and it was very cold. I lay immediately above the front entrance area and near the dormer window to young Claude's bedroom. There was a great deal of shouting, heavy footed movement in and out of the front door and throughout the house. This continued for some time and it was clear they were looking for me. They took Claude into his bedroom and began slapping him, demanding: '*Où est-il?*' (Where is he?)

I could hear the boy's reply that he knew no one and did not understand what was happening. '*Je ne connais personne.*' (I don't know anyone.) Or similar denials.

I could hear the pacing of a guard on the porch area and had the panic thought that if the Germans lost patience they had only to blaze away at the deep eaves and I would have had it.

However, this did not happen and after some time several individuals left the house and vehicles were driven away.

It was very cold in the roof but clearly I had to remain there for some time before coming out to steal some clothes and to get away again. I waited apprehensively for about three hours when I judged the house must be clear and turned quietly around to find the roof exit. The opening in the back panel to the cupboard was not easy to shift and I reached the bedroom with difficulty, moving very cautiously barefooted to find clothing and shoes.

My judgement was faulty: suddenly there was a pounding of heavy footsteps on the stairs and the door burst open to admit two men, one short and the other tall, each holding very large handguns.

Shouting and gesturing with their pistols these thugs made it abundantly clear that I was to stand in a corner with my back to them and drop my underpants, possibly to further intimidate me. It must be their intention to shoot me and I was overcome with the awful inevitability of death. The fear mounted to such a pitch that I had the thought there was little point in becoming so apprehensive.

In a flash the fear vanished and my mind emptied completely. My head had never felt so clear of concern. I awaited the worst but it never came.

After an interval, the length of which defies definition, they stepped forward, turned me round and took me to a bathroom to remove dust and other accumulated filth from the roof.

The capture was a *fait accompli* and the two men found clothing and shoes for me in the bedroom cupboard before we left the house.

This was my first encounter with the Gestapo and their rough treatment was a foretaste of what was to come.

CHAPTER 8

The Gestapo and St Gilles Prison

A small car with driver and another person was waiting for us at the front entrance. My two captors sat with me in the rear seat, their armament lying across their knees. As we drove into Brussels at around 10.00 am the questions began in French.

'*Qui êtes-vous?*' (Who are you?)

'*Je suis aviateur anglais.*' (I am an English airman)

'*Mais vous êtes en civil.*' (But you are in civilian clothes.) '*Nous vous connaissons. Vous êtes marié.*' (We know you. You are married.)

I had made a very serious mistake by speaking in French but I replied in French again and said: '*Oui c'est ça. Ma femme est enceinte.*' (Yes, it is so. My wife is pregnant.)

All four men in the car were of the German Gestapo and my two captors were French speakers. I had been able to reply to them in the same language and the way was open to them to call me a saboteur, not an airman – which they promptly did.

The journey to Brussels seemed short. We went to Gestapo headquarters in the Avenue Louise, a tall building in white stone, sandbagged along its frontage and with an SS sentry at the entrance, complete with death's-head badge on his helmet. We went up a number of floors in a lift, alighted and moved through doorways without handles. To open each door a very small aperture slid back in the wall alongside the door-frame and a voice within had to be satisfied before we were allowed through. I was eventually pushed into a tiny interrogation room, where the questioning began.

The 'treatment' was aggressive and painful and continued all morning. There was a thirty minute break in the action at the interrogators' lunch time, when I was taken down to cellar level. During that period the SS warders in charge of the heavily barred cages refused me use of a urinal so I relieved myself on the floor in their full view. I hoped they had to clean up.

Thereafter we continued with the questioning non-stop until about 7 pm. I was allowed no concessions of any kind during a very rough period lasting the whole day and my requests for the use of the lavatory or a drink of water were repeatedly rejected. The pressure was relentless and the physical treatment painful. The most heavily used threat was 'Unless you co-operate you will never see your wife again. You are a saboteur.'

At the end of the day I was exhausted and near collapse and at this point was made to sign a document alleged to be a list of my crimes. The interrogation was conducted partly in French and English and threateningly in shouted German. It was clear from the start that we had been given away. The Gestapo knew a lot about from whence I had come. Names were mentioned which I could and would not confirm. It was a long, long day in the Avenue Louise. Looking back after fifty years and with the memory of the young Royal Air Force officer caught in Iraq in the Gulf War, I probably appeared as he did, facially puffed up after the 'treatment'.

Later that evening I was taken out of the building into the backyard where a large black van awaited. I was pushed through the rear door into a narrow central corridor on both sides of which were cupboard-like cells, each having a very small window. I was pushed into one of these cells, the door of the cupboard was locked and the truck moved off.

Bruxelles St Gilles Prison is not far from the centre of the city and perhaps at a similar distance as Wormwood Scrubs is to the Old Bailey in London. We waited for the main door to open and passed into the keep where two prisoners only emerged from the black truck, myself and one other. The latter was a six-footer – as I am – and was in the full uniform of the German Wehrmacht, with decorations including the Iron Cross and shoulder rank-badges equivalent to a British Army Company Sergeant Major. He went before me into the reception room where we were ordered to strip off. My shirt, trousers, jacket and shoes were returned to me but my Air Ministry navigation watch was not. Attempts to remove a ring from the third finger of my left hand failed. The Sergeant Major was only allowed his underpants and I wondered what his offence could have been. He was a striking fellow having an aura of authority; he exchanged no remarks with the warders. I saw him once or twice much later inside the prison with mop and bucket, cleaning floors and dressed in dark grey prison garb.

I was taken through several iron-barred doors, heavily and

metallically slammed, to a cell on the ground floor in a wing supervised by the Gestapo. The cell was about six by nine feet, had a broken wood-block parquet floor, a straw-filled mattress under a window set high in the outside wall and a table which deserves special mention: it must have been a hundred years old plus. It had a heavy iron frame with thick wooden boards which had been chipped away by occupants in decades long past, leaving the surviving woodwork so damaged that it was hardly a table at all. The door slammed; my cell light, though dim, was not extinguished. Sleep was impossible that night. From now on I was truly on my own without much hope for the future, no source of help save for strength of will which, on that first night, was notably absent.

The prison came to life at 6 am with what I came to know as routine shouting. The door opened and a German soldier/warder made it clear that I should take the slop-bucket out for emptying. I refused. I let him know that I was an English officer and not prepared to perform. I managed: *'Ich bin Offizier und ein Englander.'* (I am an officer and an Englishman.)

He shouted a bit but gave up and went away returning later with a 'trusty' who removed and returned my bucket. When the warder left the cell for a few moments I asked the Belgian if he could get me a pencil and paper; he said he could but there was a price.

'Avez-vous de tabac ou des cigarettes?' (Have you any tobacco or cigarettes?)

'Oui, j'ai quelques cigarettes.' (Yes, I have some.)

A packet of cigarettes was in the pocket of my jacket taken from one of the Jeanty wardrobes. A deal was done: I gave him all the cigarettes and he promised to produce the writing material. I made him understand that I intended to write to the prison governor to seek to be released into the hands of the German military but, understandably, that information fell on deaf ears. The transaction had taken less than a minute when the warder returned. The trusty had my cigarettes and I thought I would be lucky if I ever saw him again; however, within a day or so he came back with the goods. My note to the governor sought my removal from St Gilles into the custody of the German military authorities and the letter was eventually taken away by a warder. I did not see the trusty for many days – but I had an answer from the Governor.

Two or three days later a German officer appeared and delivered a message. He said the Governor had received my note and would not take any action because as far as he was concerned I was a saboteur. I would be visited each morning by an interrogator as the Gestapo was not satisfied with what I had said. If I knew what was good for me I would answer his questions; my position would become dire if I did not co-operate. Sure enough, daily visits from another officer took place: he stood in the doorway each time and asked if I had anything else to tell him. I replied that I had not, that I was a Royal Air Force Officer. He always uttered a warning each time to the effect that this might be the last time he would visit me and that my future could not be guaranteed. These visits lasted for some seven or ten days and thereafter I heard no more. The early days of his absence did not help my morale: I had the feeling that my future had been decided.

From the second day in the prison I was taken daily to the orderly room and made to stand with a group of a dozen young men (some in uniform) all of whom had been condemned to death. I did not feel good.

One morning, at the same parade, a young prisoner in the uniform of the collaborative 'Free Belgian militia' – German support unit – muttered to me through clenched teeth an enquiry as to whom I might be.

When I replied: *'Un aviateur anglais.'*

He said: *'Ils ne vous feront rien.'* (They will do nothing to you.)

This did not comfort me for he was not an authority on which I could rely. He was able to tell me that he had been caught passing on military information to the Belgian underground movement. He had joined the militia with that intent and had been condemned to death. He appealed to me to tell his mother that he loved her but unfortunately I could not hear his name.

On one such morning parade the prison staff played sexual harassment games with one of the women warders which was not uplifting.

Extraordinarily, during this period, and throughout my confinement, I was taken weekly to the medical officer for a so-called examination. It was made up of one question *'Bist krank?'* (Are you sick?)

Each time I replied: *'Nein,'* and the 'examination' was over.

Early in my imprisonment I was transferred to a cell on the upper floor and remained there till I left St Gilles. It was to be a moderately helpful move.

Time passed slowly. A mug of ersatz coffee was thrust into the cell each morning at 6.00 am. There was often nothing to eat at midday. When something did appear it was a ladleful of potato which had been boiled to destruction with the soil unremoved. At 6.00 pm another mug of coffee arrived with a slice of heavy black bread which I always ate. I passed time by picking at the brickwork round the water pipes which ran through the walls from cell to cell just above the floor under the window. On one side I developed quite a hole. I could hear movement in the next cell and called '*Qui est là?*' (Who's there?) The occupant apparently did not wish to reply so I gave up.

Some time later I began tapping out the international call-sign 'VE' in Morse code and one day got a 'VE' response. I had found Flying Officer Brian Cooper RAF, from Santiago. We established regular contact and communicated in Morse morning and evening until other cell occupants began hitting the pipes, deliberately to wreck our daily Morse exchange. This was not before a classic exchange of stories about how we both were arrested. Brian said that he had been taken into hiding by a very active and well-armed underground group. One day, much as in my case, they were given away. The Germans surrounded the house and shooting began. His description was a laconic gem and closed with the comment – 'Bullets were flying. Acted in true British tradition: hid under bed.'

One day, after much slamming of the cell door next to mine it became clear that a new occupant had arrived. Accordingly, in due time, I called through my hole in the wall and with the best French I could muster said: '*Qui est là?*' (Who is there?)

The reply was immediate, sharp and easy to understand.

'Push off' – or words to that effect.

My reply was in similar vein but rather more colourful and it served to break the ice.

Flight Sergeant Roede, Royal Air Force, had been shot down on his first operation after a long period as an elementary flying instructor on De Havilland Tiger Moths. He had shed his uniform for civilian jacket and trousers and was promptly caught the next day. We talked twice daily and he said he had felt like weeping when he came into St Gilles prison; it had not affected me that way but I could understand. Some time later I was ordered to stand outside my cell for a moment or two and saw Roede as he stood at his cell door. He must have been at least 6 feet 2 inches tall, had a shock of red hair with a large red, giant RAF-style moustache. I thought that if he felt like weeping there was some excuse for my own no-hope beliefs.

There came a day when we were both called out of our cells to be taken for exercise. It was the first time I had left my cell for such a purpose since entering the prison six weeks before. We moved in line to the exercise area, a huge circular building divided into segments, access to each segment being gained from a small central courtyard round which were the entrances. Once inside an area one became aware, whilst the air was fresh, that there were bars at the end and overhead. Never mind, it was different and good to inhale air that others had not already used several times.

Some days later I was taken down to the ground floor for another 'exercise' and found that Roede was already waiting there. He muttered that it was the second time that morning he had been called down. We stood apart at the required distance of three paces and awaited developments. They came quickly in the shape of an unter-offizier (corporal), every scrap of 5 feet 5 inches tall. He carried a heavy baton of office and was in charge of the detail and shouted to prove it. He recognised Roede and walked quickly towards him, stopping a couple of paces away from the 6 feet 2 inch giant. Quite clearly, though speaking in German, he was saying: 'What the hell are you doing here, you've been down this morning already?' plus more histrionics for good measure.

When he stopped shouting Roede said quite simply: 'Aw, shove off!'

The little corporal knew he had been insulted and took a short step forward, lifting his baton at the same moment. Co-ordination of thought and action suddenly reminded him that Roede towered over him and he hesitated. He was so angry he lost the power to move or speak and his face showed graphic signs of apoplexy. Roede and I and the little German knew he had lost the skirmish. Another warder escorted us back to our cells. I lost valuable fresh air but it mattered not at all – it was all worth it, every pfennig!

Looking back on those sixty-five days and nights of solitary confinement I wonder about my state of mind at the time. Boredom was not a problem: I would certainly have argued with St Paul in 1 Corinthians 13.13 where he says 'And so abideth faith, hope and charity, these three, but the greatest of these is charity.' I concentrated a little more on faith and hope. The time went by because I let it do so and because my front-runner was hope. I was a very long way from optimism and there were really no grounds for hope save for the fact that I was still breathing. Charity was certainly not in the frame in my prison cell. I did physical exercises, paced the cell, worried desperately about Mary at home, the Jeantys and the Gestapo interrogation. It was a pretty hostile environment and I tried to determine in what mental state I could be. It seemed to be akin to a vacuum.

The prison sounds marked the time of day so one was able to determine the hour, more or less. When I went for lightning medical examinations I was able to take a look at the faces of other inmates and knew that I was not the only one in trouble by a very long way. The sight of some prisoners wearing a Ku Klux Klan hood of sacking disturbed me a lot. Clearly it was meant to keep secret the identity of the prisoner under the hood. I would go back to my cell, putting together other constructions on the purpose of hoods. In this context it was grim to hear, in the very early hours of some mornings, the sound of slamming cell doors and cries of 'Vive la Belgique.'

There was little doubt that the worst was about to happen to some poor fellow. It took some time to be rid of those sounds and that cry.

My neighbour and friend, the Flight Sergeant, moved out and my line to Brian Cooper, via the water pipe, was jammed by other prisoners. I was in another time phase. But then it happened: one morning a German SS soldier entered the cell and handed over my Air Ministry watch. I had to sign for it. He left without a word. What could this mean? Surely if they were going to shoot me there was no need to return my watch?

The answer came in the afternoon. I was taken down to the ground floor and put in a cell bare of any furniture. Over the next thirty minutes four other men entered the cell clad in an assortment of RAF battledress uniform or RAF trousers with various civilian upper garments. Not a word was spoken for fifteen minutes when, suddenly, there burst out a cry from one of the newcomers: 'What the bloody hell is this? I'm an English airman – what are you lot? I don't care if this is a plant!'

All five of us were shot-down fliers, about to begin a journey to Frankfurt-on-Main, the Luftwaffe Interrogation Centre.

We were led out of the prison, climbed into a truck and were taken to a train under heavy guard. The German authorities categorised me as dangerous and for this reason I had to be manacled. I tolerated this with no difficulty – I was out of St Gilles and had a future. I had done sixty-five days solitary – if I ever got back home I would never even break the speed limit. I knew the awfulness of a prison cell.

The rail carriage was a corridor type and outside each seating compartment a sentry with a submachine gun was posted. Other compartments were filled with US Army Air Corps aviators. All windows were criss-crossed with barbed wire and we were warned that if, during the journey, anyone attempted to escape he would be shot. The Germans left nothing to chance.

The journey was to take twenty-four hours. We had our first sightings of cattle trucks crammed with people, limp hands waving pitifully through high openings in the truck sides. We were told not to look at these trucks. We knew they must be bound for concentration camps but gas chambers were not in our vocabulary until much later in our lives.

Detrainment took place at the Interrogation camp, Dulag Luft, at Oberursel near Frankfurt-on-Main and, very soon, each man went into a narrow cell with a straw palliassed cot and a large radiator. A Luftwaffe intelligence officer, a captain, paid me an early visit and left a Red Cross Form for me to complete. He returned the next day and requested the form which remained untouched.

'You know I can't fill that in.'

'You need have no inhibition about completing it.'

'I have an officer's military inhibition about completing it.'

'Perhaps this will help you.'

He produced a sheet of paper on which, in pencil, there was written my curriculum vitae in the Royal Air Force. Every posting and every date was there. I gave it back to him and shrugged my shoulders; I was speechless and shaken by its accuracy.

Questions about my flight on the night of 11/12 June followed and he was keen to know how the Radar navigation instrument ('Gee') performed on the night of the Düsseldorf operation. I recalled that we had been briefed that a modification to combat German jamming had been made to 'Gee' which, it was said, would carry radar signals further beyond the European coast but it proved useless on the night. I refused to answer the question. My interrogator said that unless I answered I would stay in the cell and life would become uncomfortable for me; he would return the next day. Soon after he left the radiator began to heat up and the cell became very hot. I did not find it intolerable so, when he returned the next day, I still had nothing to say. The treatment continued until the following day. When he came in I said that 'Gee' had operated much further into European airspace and he was happy and I was happy. It was not true – the so-called new addition to 'Gee' was a dead loss.

I was also made content when I was released from the cell and joined other Allied and American aircrew prisoners of war. They were in uniform; I was the odd man out it seemed.

The Senior British Officer (SBO) at Frankfurt was a squadron leader, who must have been long-serving in that rank when he became a prisoner. He had been SBO for some time and vicious rumour had it that he remained at Frankfurt because he was favoured by the Germans.

During 1944 when I was at the Belaria Lager of Stalag Luft 3 in Sagan, this squadron leader joined us there, when these rumours were revived. However, the SBO of Belaria, Group Captain J.C. Macdonald, chose well when he issued a statement concerning this officer. It conveyed very clearly that the rumours about him should be killed off and that there was emphatically no reason to suspect that he had conducted himself in any way other than as a loyal and faithful individual.

This newcomer shared a room with another senior squadron leader, Tim Piper, in the HQ Block where I was located and he became a popular member of prisoner society. (At the end of the war a quite different officer was tried and executed for passing on information within the Dulag at Oberursel.)

When we travelled eastward from Frankfurt to Stalag Luft 3 in Lower Silesia, we witnessed more movements of people by cattle-truck. Similar pale faces and limp hands showed through openings high in the sides of the trucks. We were held in the railway yard at Leipzig especially long and were placed quite near these dreadful transporters. A warning came from the guards yet again not to look but it was impossible to avoid the sight. It is inescapable that knowledge of this dreadful activity must have been widespread within the civilian and military communities in Germany.

The rail journey was protracted and lasted two days and nights.

Unquestionably bombing had caused rail detours and substantial delays to progress. We were heavily guarded throughout; the guards never relaxed. My manacles were removed when I adjourned to the lavatory but restored upon my return to my seat.

CHAPTER 9

Stalag Luft 3 – Centre Compound

In company with half a dozen Commonwealth Air Force members and rather more Americans from the US Army Air Corps, I reached the Stalag at Sagan in early November 1943. Flight Lieutenant John Bridger DFC had been kind to me during the journey for I was in bad physical shape, starved and finding most of my joints painful. The Americans, also kind, named me the 'Gestapo Kid' – fortunately this soubriquet did not last.

Our names were taken as we entered the Centre Compound of the Stalag. We would have been 'logged in' the movement book kept by a duty prisoner-of-war; his position at a window in a neighbouring block enabled him to observe all comings and goings through the main gate. This record was kept for reasons of inmates' (Allied personnel) security, it being essential always to know how many German security men, 'Goons' or 'ferrets', were in the compound at any moment of time. This measure served especially to protect POW escape activity, or any other related matters which needed to be kept out of sight.

We met the Senior British Officer (SBO), a certain Squadron Leader Jennings whose general attitude to young wartime officers was condescending and disdainful. John Bridger and I joined a group of twelve fellow Royal Air Force Officers in one of seven or eight wooden barrack blocks. Arthur Strudwick (now a retired Air Commodore), Peter Kingsford-Smith (a nephew of the famous Australian aviator), Kingsley Brown (one-time editor of one of Nova Scotia's newspapers) and Tommy Lowry (one-time scrum-half for the Wasps RFC) were among my new companions.

Douglas Bader, also in Centre Compound, was about to be removed to Colditz; he had become a nuisance and left almost immediately. He would throw stones at the German soldiers patrolling the perimeter fences and perform other useless nuisance measures. Punishments were wreaked upon the whole prisoner population within the compound and no one mourned his departure.

I met one of the members of the POW security committee, a Squadron Leader Hughes DSO DFC whose task it was to de-brief me and to establish my bona fides. At the conclusion of the meeting he asked me if I would be prepared to take part in the escaping activity within the compound. My reply was that I would help with any effort but did not care to escape myself. He asked me why not? I said I had had enough of escaping for the time being. I was too preoccupied with thoughts for the safety of people who had helped me in my attempts to escape to feel very keen on making another attempt, also I needed to get fit again. I do not believe this reply was the one he wanted. However, I was concerned and later had a talk with the padre, expressing my anxiety and state of mind. The message that came back from the SBO via the padre showed a degree of understanding.

My part in the camp routine began at once. There were two assemblies (appels) on the open space in the centre of the lager/ compound. First appel was 0830 hours and the second in late afternoon, depending on the time of year. The square was surrounded by armed Luftwaffe soldiers, placed to prevent the deliberate and/or mischievous drifting off of prisoners intent on confusing the counting of heads. Once the figures were agreed the parade was dismissed. At that time the intake of American aircrew substantially exceeded Allied aircrew. The SBO was soon replaced as compound leader by a Senior Allied Officer (SAO), a Southern States US Army Air Corps Colonel Spivey. He was an elderly gentleman, a gunnery expert who had been shot down on a mission undertaken to show him how things worked in practice on daylight raids.

Soon after becoming Senior Allied Officer he called a special appel and it became clear that he was very angry.

He said on that very day he had washed his shirt in the wash-house and in so doing removed his command pilot's flying badge from above the left-breast pocket and placed it on the bench alongside. When he finished the job and prepared to leave with his shirt he could not find his wings badge. It would have had particular value as a gem-decorated silver item.

His concluding words from a basic vocabulary fell like a lead balloon on unbelieving RAF officers' ears, censored and approximated as follows: 'Among you officers and gentlemen there is a son-of-a-bitch who has snitched ma wings. Ah will take no action if it is returned to me immediately. This is a goddam low-down trick by a no-good bastard.' Spoken as an officer and a gentleman! Its delivery and content were a surprise and a shock. I had never before heard such a level of public expression.

The badge was never recovered, but it was certainly a dirty trick by a so-called officer amongst our ranks.

One had to undertake one's share of daily chores: carrying hot water and whatever food the Germans issued, mostly boiled barley, heavy dark bread (one slice per man), a small amount of margarine weekly and preparing other food supplied in Red Cross parcels.

The barrack blocks and occupied rooms had also to be kept in reasonable order. Two-tier bunks were provided and much later displaced by three tiers as the influx of prisoners grew.

After a month of this régime, in early December 1943, I was called to the SBO's quarters. Jennings had been replaced by a Wing Commander who said the Gestapo had instructed the Stalag Luft 3 authorities to take me back to Brussels for further interrogation. There would also be a 'confrontation'. He had protested, for under the Geneva Convention on the care of prisoners, this treatment was absolutely unacceptable. He had been told that the Gestapo's wishes had to be obeyed and I was to leave the next day but I need not answer any more questions about my period of evasion. He said he was sorry that I had to undergo this trip and wished me well.

This development was a shaker. There had been time to get the prison and the Gestapo partly out of my system. Now I was to go back into the thick of it all over again 'to the scene of my crimes', this being the definition of my return by the Gestapo.

I left Sagan by train under escort of three men, two senior Luftwaffe feldwebels (sergeants) and an interpreter, a Luftwaffe gefreiter (lance-corporal). Our compartment was reserved and once seated I was told that they were ready to allow me a choice so far as their own and my travel comfort was concerned. They had been ordered to keep me handcuffed, but if I sat in a corner seat away from the door and undertook not to escape or give them trouble they would forget the handcuffs. If I attempted to escape, handcuffed or not, they would shoot me. I accepted the deal and sat in the corner with the interpreter, facing the two fifty year-old grey-haired sergeants.

The interpreter and I talked in English a little as the journey proceeded. He told me he handled the outward and inward prisoner mail and had served within the confines of Stalag Luft 3 for some time. He was a friendly fellow and especially so when he said the three of them knew I was going back to prison to face the Gestapo again and to take part in a confrontation – an identity parade. He went on: 'You do not have to answer any questions; you are a registered prisoner-of-war and you can exercise your rights in this matter. Moreover, you are to be questioned by the Gestapo and none of us like them. You need have no inhibitions in behaving in this way.'

This advice almost matched that given me by the SBO and I was much encouraged. We exchanged views generally and on one occasion were warned by the senior sergeant not to talk so much – possibly when it might have appeared that I was enjoying the conversation! The journey was not done at speed; there were delays which, from the conversations in German, I deduced that the railway had been hit by bombing.

After several hours the interpreter asked me how long I had been a prisoner and when I had been shot down. I answered both questions giving him the date as 11 to 12 June of that year, 1943.

'That must have been Düsseldorf, was it not?'

'Yes,' I answered.

'That was the night my parents' house and my own home were destroyed. My family had a factory which was also razed to the ground.'

'I hope your parents were not injured.'

'No, they are well. My mother is meeting this train at Düsseldorf station. I have not seen her for many months and am looking forward to the meeting. I then have to go on with you to Brussels.'

Nothing more was said on this issue and later we pulled into Düsseldorf. The station had no roof and destruction encircled it. In a few moments the interpreter was out of the train and quickly found his mother who had been waiting several hours. For as long as he could he talked within sight of the three of us on the train. When the train began to move he returned to our compartment with a package tied up in a white napkin. When undone, four packed meals were revealed and I remember the food was very good.

I thanked my travelling companion warmly. This kindness set me back on my heels somewhat and all that I could deduce was that I had found a good German family and that there had to be more. The slogan on a German serviceman's belt buckle *'Gott mit uns'* (God with us) must have meaning for some people. The next morning we arrived in Brussels and I was delivered to prison.

I was soon back in a cell in St Gilles prison – with an important difference: I was in RAF blue battledress. Moreover, on that very day I was visited by a German Army officer, a Hauptmann (captain) who gave me a standard salute and told me of the Governor's regret that there was no other accommodation available. It was a difficult time to find accommodation in Brussels and he hoped that I would not remain long in prison. So saying he saluted again and the door slammed. It was certainly different this time – so far.

My stay lasted two weeks during which I was taken three times by road to Louvain and motored round the streets there. I genuinely did not, in fact, recognise any area we visited and was asked no questions. Each trip took about two hours and was welcome in that I liked the sight of the open country. Each time the car carried five persons, myself and four plain-clothed Gestapo men. Those not driving had their pistols held on their knees and I wondered what would happen if I suddenly screamed.

Would there be an accident with the guns, when possibly the reproductive capability of the guards might be destroyed! A preposterous thought, particularly as I might also be damaged!

We witnessed an American Flying Fortress daylight raid on a Belgian airfield. The car screamed to a stop and, save for myself, everyone leapt into the ditch. I was left alone for a few moments until my absence was noticed! They came quickly back to the car, dragged me out and threw me into the ditch. Minutes later I was allowed to watch the bombing from the bank and alongside a Belgian road-worker.

Those three trips were the aggregate of my activity whilst back in gaol. No questions were asked and there was no 'confrontation' with anyone, Gestapo or otherwise. Something had been achieved however: two senior NCOs had been taken away from their jobs and an interpreter's time had been lost on the journey to and from Brussels.

Back at the prison, halfway through my stay there, I gained a cell-mate. The door was flung open and a tall fellow was pushed in; he wore fawn coloured US Army Air Corps trousers, decorated calf-length cowboy boots, a blue Eagle Squadron silk scarf and a blue battle-jacket. We were intensely suspicious of each other; my immediate reaction was that he was a 'plant' and his feeling was obviously the same. His accent worried me for it was a combination of French and American. His name was Ed Stanhope and he was a lieutenant in the US Army Air Corps.

At the outset of our exchanges we were very cautious but as the remaining days of my stay in the prison went by we gained confidence in each other. I told my story and described what he was to expect both at the Frankfurt Dulag Interrogation Centre and Stalag Luft 3. I remarked upon his silk scarf and his splendid wrist watch and told him that both these would be confiscated when he got to Sagan. I added that there was the strongest of possibilities that he would come into the Centre Compound where both Allied and American airmen officers were housed. With that in mind I suggested that I take back the above-mentioned possessions and make sure that they were returned to him when he arrived. There was little likelihood that I would be searched when I returned and a greater chance that he could keep possession of the two items. Quite understandably he found this idea difficult to accept, but close to the time of my departure he took the plunge and agreed. It was risky but well worth a try.

Now into December I began my journey back to Sagan. We were three in number, the same two sergeants but no interpreter; he had already returned to Sagan. I was given to understand that the same rules applied if I wore no handcuffs. The journey eastwards was slow and took quite a different route. We were to go via Berlin and change there for a train to Breslau, stopping at Sagan. It took the whole of the first day to run across the central plain of Germany to reach Berlin near midnight. So far we had again travelled in a reserved compartment. I cannot remember the name of the Berlin station where we alighted, but it must have been Friedrichstrasse. What I do recall were dense crowds on the platforms and the noise of steam locomotives arriving and departing, each having the slogan on the front of the engine: 'We will go on until victory.' At the same time an air-raid was in progress and close by anti-aircraft guns were firing.

The two sergeants gripped my arms very firmly as we waited for our Breslau train for Sagan. When it arrived they sought our compartment and found it easily by sighting the usual white window reservation sticker. With all the other would-be passengers, we made our move to board the train. Immediately there were objections and an argument started between the two Luftwaffe men and a number of passengers; I was not to be allowed on the train and it made no difference that the compartment was *reserviert* as it was already occupied by other travellers. We withdrew from argument and awaited our opportunity. Other passengers waiting on the platform became menacing; my blue battledress and the general disturbance had attracted their attention. At this point the sergeants drew their pistols and we climbed onto the open connecting stage between two carriages. As Wellington said of Waterloo, 'It was a near run thing.'

Despite the pistols we were not allowed into a compartment and I was to remain on the moving link in the open air for the eight hour journey to Sagan. It was a bitterly cold night and soon my hands, gripping brass hand-rails, were locked on with the cold. I had no greatcoat and was shaking in the freezing atmosphere. The two guards, my friends by then, took turns to stand on the wooden staging to watch whether or not I fell off – or tried an escape perhaps! I appreciated their presence all the way to Sagan.

On entering the Stalag guard-room I was given the usual ersatz coffee and had to listen to an impassioned argument, dominated by a Nazi party member, about the Italian surrender – the Führer had been so brilliant in holding on to the Italian navy after the armistice. It was quite heated with the Nazi providing the fuel!

A period of waiting in a cell in the cooler followed to await admittance to Centre Compound. The journey had been very wearing and the life-like drawing of a nude girl on the wall next to the bunk, executed by a gifted and frustrated prisoner, failed to interest me or to reduce the clear memory of the events of the preceding forty-eight hours. I think I said: 'Bloody hell.'

When back inside I reported at once to the Wing Commander and told him of my encounter with Ed Stanhope. He listened carefully, was happy with the outcome and welcomed me back. I deposited Ed's scarf and watch with Colonel Spivey, the Senior Allied Officer (SAO) and rejoined my room-mates and hoped to settle down, but it was not to happen quickly.

One of our colleagues, Gerry Collis, gave us a bad night as he developed acute peritonitis. The guards were called and he was taken speedily to hospital. Two French army surgeons who were also in captivity performed the operation and one could not fault the speed with which the German military had responded. Otherwise the routine continued.

It was inevitable that the feeling of restriction and loss of liberty behind high fences should be fully revived in me again. There was no landscape view to provide balm to the eyes beyond the wire because deep pine forest over flat country intervened. One walked round the compound circuit time after time; the monotony continued, but the human spirit was at work in the background of the community mind to provide relief.

Theatre seating in an empty hut was being built out of used Red Cross food parcel boxes, rugby was being played on the sandy parade ground, Pete Brewer practised hypnosis, plays such as *Rope* and *French without Tears* were in rehearsal, the newly-formed orchestra was tuning up in true Glenn Miller style and a choir was practising: all these efforts were for Christmas showing. One got on with life as it presented itself. In retrospect one has to remember that all hope was being extinguished at Auschwitz not too far away.

Ed Stanhope arrived in the compound, collected his watch and Eagle Squadron scarf and eventually appeared in one of the shows, a revue, as a woman, dressed most slinkily! He sang '*J'attendrai, j'attendrai toujours*' alluringly, to whoops and whistles of delight from an audience in enforced celibacy.

There came a time when I saw the German interpreter again as he came into the compound with a trug full of mail. It was against internal POW rules for those other than appointed German speakers to converse with German personnel, but I owed the man some thanks. I walked a few strides with him and said quickly that I appreciated his help. This was witnessed by one Flight Lieutenant Christopher Cheshire, brother of the great man Leonard. He reported me to the SBO and I was summoned to call on him immediately. I explained and the Wing Commander waved me away.

'Forget it, Harris,' said he. 'It's nothing.' He grinned through his momentary impatience.

There were other events which are worthy of mention. The first was a full-scale debate on the motion that 'Western Civilization is decadent'. It seemed to me that the whole of the German Kommandantur attended, assembled in the front row of the audience. The motion was lost. I am bound to reflect on what might happen today if such a proposition was put to the same or a similar gathering of intelligent young men, made worldly wise by extreme events. It is inescapable that the proposition would be bound to succeed.

An explosive development started early one morning with the appearance, in force, of the German guards in each of the barrack blocks.

'*Raus, raus, appel, appel, raus!*' they shouted as they entered, opening all the doors down the central corridor and yelling as they went. Immediately the word went round that we were not to hurry and some retired again to their bunks. But the guards were especially impatient, insistent and angry and came through again threatening with staccato sentences in which '*Kuhler*' (Cooler) could be heard.

Within moments there was the sound of a sub-machine gun. Those who were not already up and on their way to the appel leapt out of any crevice or gap in the building including doors and windows, in a frenzied movement to safety on the parade ground.

The word was soon out thereafter. There had been an escape from the East Compound next to us and our delaying tactics slowed the urgent attempts to count us. They feared that somehow there had been escapes from both compounds, but their anxiety was misplaced. After the appel a number of prisoners stood at the fences near the gateway to the compound and jeered the guards as they left. I watched this mini-drama from a distance and witnessed the sudden loss of patience by the Germans. They had assembled into a section of forty men and were ordered, very sharply indeed, to about-turn and bring their armament to bear on the mob.

I have never seen men move so quickly from a scene. A touch more anger and the control would have been lost by shooting. Unknowingly we had all played a part in the closing scenes of 'The Wooden Horse' escape. Escaper Eric Williams' book is still a good read.

Oberst (Colonel) von Lindemann, the Stalag Luft Commandant, was sacked. He was a very senior officer of the old school and delighted in bringing in his two dachshunds whenever he attended an appel. He was replaced by a party man with a large German shepherd dog. The dachshunds got the odd boot from some of the more vicious officer and gentleman members of the prisoner fraternity, but the alsatian looked as dangerous and offensive as his master, both of whom were given a wide berth.

Christmas 1943 was not far off when, much to our surprise, the

Germans sent in half a dozen very large barrels of beer. Each of the six barrack blocks was allocated a barrel. The beer was very light and was consumed fairly rapidly up to and including the festive season. During the latter period it was one of two additions to our normal diet; the second was a so-called Christmas cake, the contents of which defy both description and memory.

The empty beer barrels stood around and stimulated thoughts and crystallised plans of an attempt to escape by six of the shortest prisoners. Clearly, if the barrels could be adapted to admit a small body then it was worth a try. Permission was sought from the Escape Committee and the project was agreed.

It fell to my room-mates and me to do the job for our barrack-block. The work had to be done quickly for it was certain that collection would be made soon after Christmas. We set to work enthusiastically with German issue table knives which had almost no cutting edge and not much leverage capability. We had to remove at least two of the four iron hoops which held the barrel together. When this was done, one barrel-end had to be reduced in radius and substantially bevelled around its new circumference in order that it could be pushed back into position from inside the cask. There it was held by two sticks lodged into tiny carved recesses in the side of the barrel. The reduction of the diameter of the circular barrel-end and its bevelling was very difficult and tedious until one bright spark among our colleagues successfully converted two of our knives into small saws. The new teeth helped a great deal and reduced the number of blistered hands. During the day the barrels had to stand on their tampered ends with hoops restored. Work recommenced as soon as curfew time closed all barrack-blocks.

Two or three nights after Christmas the work on our barrel was finished. Tommy Lowry proposed to have a dummy run in the barrel, wearing all the kit he proposed to take with him. He climbed in, propped up the barrel end in position and we rolled the barrel up and down the corridor. Eventually a muffled cry came from within: 'Okay, stop rolling, I'm ready.'

We stood the barrel on end and everything went smoothly until Tom got out of the barrel. He was completely drunk and could just keep upright – but not on the move! The warmth of his body had released alcohol fumes from the wood which had lain there for many years – and they zonked him absolutely! I have never laughed so much as on that occasion. Moreover, I cannot remember discussing what would have happened to an escaper if the barrels, when taken away, were stacked the wrong way up. To be under the influence of alcohol fumes and positioned upside down does not bear thinking about!

When the German brewer arrived for his barrels they were rolled out to the collection point. Sadly, one occupant got into difficulty and stood up in his barrel! It was all up with the venture and six prisoners went to the cooler. The brewer's drayman wept as he surveyed his once beautiful but comprehensively ruined barrels!

There was another amusing event. The padre had secured the agreement of the Germans that a small working party of prisoners might go to the area outside the bounds of the Stalag where deceased prisoners had been buried; there they gave attention to weeding and other tasks in the small cemetery. During their work some children came to watch and the opportunity was taken to educate them. They were to repeat it when they returned home. It went something like this: 'Three cheers for Winston Churchill. Three cheers for President Roosevelt. Up Hitler for a bag of nuts!'

The cat was very quickly out of the bag and the group did fourteen days in the cooler. They had given their parole not to escape but felt free to disseminate general goodwill instead!

The most significant event in my life at that time was the receipt of a letter from Mary in February 1944. It told of the arrival of our first-born, Catherine Sandra. A photograph of mother and baby was enclosed. I must have read the letter and looked at the picture a hundred times on the first day of their arrival.

One of our pastimes was to play rugby and we found out how painful it was to be block tackled by opposing Americans playing the game for the first time. The pain comes when going at full tilt and the block tackle is applied. The lower half of the body stops but the upper wants to go on further! I refereed games and on one occasion had to stop a game when an unacceptable level of criticism of my decisions was reached. The most vociferous individual was a Welsh nonconformist lay-reader whom I had to tell to pack up or I would send him off. It worked!

We sang 'Rule Britannia' lustily at the end of shows in the theatre because national anthems were forbidden. I sang tenor in the choir and attended Holy Communion services held in the theatre.

I talked long with Royal Air Force NCOs whose duties covered kitchen and other support duties at the behest of the German authorities. They were RAF career men and individuals of particular quality. The war had robbed them of their freedom, their pay and promotion and their seniority. Moreover, they had weathered being prisoners from the early days of the war when the treatment from the enemy was brutal. They were men who might have reached high office in the RAF had they not been shot down. Their luckier colleagues enjoyed that achievement in a great many cases.

An ugly incident in early 1944 has also to be recorded. Throughout the day many circuits of the whole compound were made by the population, all seeking exercise and fresh air by the only means possible. The compound was surrounded by a double fence four metres in height. Between those two fences lay rolled barbed wire and five yards from the innermost of the two, into the compound, there was a post and warning rail standing a little over a metre high; if one trespassed beyond this rail one would certainly be shot.

One fine day two friends were walking round the perimeter, one of whom was trailing his right hand along the top of the warning rail. A *posten* (sentry) in one of the elevated observation towers noticed this 'breach' of the rules, lifted his rifle, aimed and shot the young man through the hand. Miraculously the bullet entered the hand just below the joint of the fourth finger and passed under the skin of the palm of the hand and exited below the index joint and the thumb. Action was immediate: the wounded man was dealt with jointly by the resident POW doctor and the German medical staff. The sentry was removed at once and was posted, so we were told, to the Eastern Front. We did not wish him well.

CHAPTER 10

Stalag Luft 3 - Belaria

Within a couple of months of Christmas 1943 all RAF and Commonwealth officers were ordered to prepare their kit for departure to another location within the ambit of Stalag Luft 3. Centre Compound had been taking in a steady flow of American aircrew and the compound would henceforward take in US Air Corps only. All other nationalities were in a minority and the latter were divided into two parties, one to go to North Compound and the other to Belaria, situated a few kilometres distant from the main prison camp area. We lost some new friends including Kingsley Brown, the Canadian ex-journalist, to whom I would next speak in 1990 by telephone at his home in Nova Scotia from my hotel in Halifax. He was much older than me and at eighty-six failed to remember me.

But I gained another acquaintance in the person of Harold Dothie, a man whose height was six feet three inches and of substantial build. Like almost everyone else he had parachuted to stay alive but landed in an electricity power-generating station within a restricted, specially highly-charged area, surrounded by a very high fence: he had two very narrow escapes in a very short space of time. The long arm of Tatsfield reached out to Belaria and touched both of us. His brother Bill and sister-in-law were customers of my father and before I was shot down I learned from my parents that Bill had won a Military Cross. He took an opportunity to run swiftly from a marching column of British prisoners in Northern France in 1940 and made it back to England – an exciting family indeed!

Belaria was atop a long rise out of Sagan alongside a straight stretch of road in open country. It was said to be escape-proof and proved to be so, save for one intrepid prisoner named Charles Ellis who impulsively rolled himself up in a tarpaulin on a delivery truck within the compound and got away for about twenty-four hours. On his return he was reprimanded for escaping without the agreement of the Escape Committee. An early manifestation of bureaucracy perhaps, but to go through channels was out of the question in the circumstances.

I was assigned to a room in the SBO's Headquarters barrack block with most of my Centre Compound friends, Messrs Strudwick (Flight Lieutenant and later in life to be RAF Officer Commanding the Rocket Range at Woomera in Australia and an Air Commodore) and Lowry, Huntley, Gosling, Kelly, Collis and Bennett (Flying Officers). The compound was much smaller than Centre Compound and the circuit walk shorter accordingly. Appel took place on the broad path along the boundary fence near the main gate. It was cold, very cold; the strong winds swept through the camp having come at top speed from Greater Russia including Siberia. We were soon joined by a small party of prisoners from North Compound. Those who have read books and seen television documentaries about 'The Great Escape' will know their names – as will others: Robert Stanford-Tuck, Wally Floody, George Harsh and Fanshawe, a Fleet Air Arm officer, all of whom were banished to Belaria because the Germans suspected they were key figures in escape activity in North Compound. The construction of tunnels had been masterminded by Wally Floody, a prominent participant and chief engineer.

As the weeks went by, activity in all departments went on apace. The flow of British and Commonwealth captured aircrew continued; a college was formed by Harold Eyre (later to become Head of the Adult Education Department in Cardiff) and I signed up as an elementary French teacher. The record and book libraries grew, plays began to rehearse, a myriad of seven-a-side football teams were formed (including Hetero versus Homo).

I was appointed a censor of outgoing mail of all prisoners up to the rank of Flight Lieutenant. Tim Piper appointed me and I was surprised he chose me as I was barely twenty-two years old. Piper was a very senior squadron leader (who, post-war, became Air Marshal Sir Timothy Piper) and was No. 2 to the SBO, Group Captain MacDonald.

Tim was also Mr 'X' in Belaria which denoted that he was Chairman of the Escape and Security Committee. This committee oversaw all clandestine activities including the building and operation of a radio to receive Allied news broadcasts. I recall being told of the shortage of a vital part in the building of this radio. Somehow a message was successfully carried to North Compound telling of this shortage. Group Captain Massie, the Senior British

Officer in that compound and for the Stalag, contrived to pay an official visit to Belaria in that role. He was transported by the German authorities and successfully hid the much needed valve or condenser or both in his flying boots. Thus it was that our keeping up to date resumed and the radio set survived many searches by our captors.

Spring came and in May the flying bugs were absolutely enormous. Attempts were made to race these large insects with a small paper strip attached, but the idea failed.

The sun shone for long periods and brown bodies were everywhere. Nude sun-bathing began but was halted when the SBO ordered it to stop, the practice being defined as 'aesthetically distasteful'.

A group of tiny allotments was developed in a little used corner of the compound and successful attempts were made to grow tomatoes and pumpkins from seeds sent in by the International Red Cross. Budding gardeners grew tomatoes which had a very acceptable flavour in our tasteless existence; others grew pumpkins and at the appropriate moment performed surgery on the fruit. A section was cut out, some sugar inserted and the hole was replugged, only to be withdrawn for further additions of sugar. I understood at the time that the liquid obtained in the autumn had flavour, sweetness and contained alcohol.

Cy Grant, a West Indian officer and a very proficient guitarist, charmed us all with his playing and his personality. In his later years he became a professional entertainer, joining the 'Blue Peter' children's television show.

Another less popular musician came into possession of some bagpipes and began to practise in the wash-house. Some patience was exercised by the community but this soon ran out and the piper was threatened with murder if he continued! A compromise was reached where he blew straight into the instrument without the bag. The sound was suitably muted and tolerated!

One boundary fence lay along the road and interested prisoners whistled as German girls cycled past. This extra-curricular passive activity was snuffed out by the erection of a boarded fence which blotted out the passing scenery!

The last, and almost successful, assassination attempt on Hitler took place and we began to get radio news of it from UK through the camp-built set. As a gesture of loyalty to the Führer the German officers were ordered to use the Nazi party salute instead of the imperial version. Strictly speaking we were supposed to salute any German officer of equal rank or above but never normally did so. However, when this order became known and very evident, we made a point of saluting and received the Nazi salute in return! German officers soon became exhausted and the practice ceased almost at once!

Barrack-block searches took place regularly and on one such occasion it was discovered that the SBO had a large supply of clandestinely distilled hooch which he claimed was for medicinal use only – a likely story! It was all seized by the searchers.

At about that time Oberfeldwebel Glemnitz was appointed as chief German Security Officer. He was a particularly effective operator amongst his own people as well as the prisoners. His team of Goons were on patrol during daylight hours and at night-time with a German shepherd dog. They crawled under the barrack blocks to seek evidence of tunnel digging and prodded the ground near the perimeter fencing with long spikes for the same reason. In these activities they achieved the soubriquet of 'ferrets', for their enquiring look was not unlike the pointed muzzle of that animal. Knowledge of the number of ferrets in the compound was most important to us, as the degree of risk at any important moment in illegal prisoner activity could then be established.

In the spring of 1944 I went down badly with persistent asthma and spent periods in the sick bay in the care of Doc Monteuuis (Twee), a British Army doctor from Eastbourne, and his small team of POW medical students. When not unwell I assisted in the sick quarters and here spent some time in the company of Wing-Co Robert Stanford-Tuck when we were both in-patients. He was a very amusing man, suave, authoritative and an ace pilot. He made much of his personally prepared dessert, sweetened boiled barley with milk powder added and claimed that the delicate flavour of burn was an experience not to be missed! Indeed, he suspected that his presence in the sick-quarters was a hell of a relief to his room-mates!

I found it instructive when I acted as the Doc's clerk when the morning sick-parade took place. Complaints from would-be patients about their tiresome cough would evoke the reply:

'You should hear mine!' and he would cough quite violently when standing close to the patient. 'Go and do some breathing exercises and come back and see me when you're better.'

He was a doctor for all seasons, men and moods. Encouraging here and speaking toughly there and he knew his business even to the point where he had a burly Canadian fellow bending over to display a grimy bottom in a search for haemorrhoids!

'A bit messy round here,' says Twee.

'Whaddya expect – ice-cream?' says the patient.

One day the German doctor brought in a very sick Royal Canadian Air Force pilot who had been held in a German medical unit. His illness had not been diagnosed, but Doc Monteuuis did not take long to pronounce on young Mackenzie's condition: it was Hodgkinson's Disease or leukaemia. I was one of a number of assistants in the sick quarters who attended him. We corresponded after the war, but sadly he died. His last letter said that he was 'not able to see far into the future'.

Later in the year we were profoundly shocked and angered by the news of the shooting of fifty fellow Royal Air Force Officers following the escape of seventy-four prisoners from the North Compound. A memorial service was held on the small football area, closely surrounded by guards bearing machine-guns. Rumour had it that they were fearful of our anger and that this might persuade us to make a mass break-out. Relations with all German personnel were reduced to near zero. My friend Denis Street was one of the fifty officers murdered by the Gestapo.

Coincidentally, our local vicar today, the Reverend Hamilton Lloyd, trained as a pilot with Denis in Oklahoma. The world can be a small place sometimes – happily or sadly.

Near this time Belaria was visited by a Swiss Medical Board, the purpose of which was to establish medically whether any prisoners were sick or wounded seriously enough to warrant repatriation. Doc Monteuuis put young Mackenzie and me forward and we were both judged to be worthy of a green ticket for the next exchange of prisoners between the Allies and the Germans. I was in luck! So was Mac, but sadly it was heavily diluted.

At the end of the summer concessions were made by the Kommandantur which allowed prisoners into an adjoining fenced field on parole and it was here that a series of Test Matches was played between England and Australia (captained by Keith Carmody, later to be Captain of South Australia and a member of the Australian Team in the end-of-war Test Matches at Lords). England lost the Tests in Belaria – a result that fortunately does not qualify for Wisden!

There were one or two cases of complete nervous collapse and one attempted suicide which failed. The Germans had offered a series of walks outside the compound. We had to give our parole that we would not attempt to escape; if an attempt was made the escaper would be shot. Shortly after the departure of one party, a letter from one of the walkers was found, addressed to the SBO. It stated that the individual would run away from the party, deliberately to invite the inevitable action from the guards. Group Captain Macdonald contacted the local German commandant and immediate action was taken to catch up with the walkers before the attempt took place. They really moved fast and reached the group in time. He had gone beyond the limits of his tolerance of prison life. I knew the lad quite well and felt keenly for him, as many others did also.

The summer weather had been good and we were thrilled and heartened both by the Normandy invasion and the Russian progress on the Eastern Front, but shattered by the disaster at Arnhem later on in the campaign. The winter returned on one night in early October as if a switch had been turned. It was bitterly cold and soon there was a substantial depth of snow over the land.

The Germans chose this moment to fumigate one of the blocks as a de-lousing and de-bed-bugging measure. The occupants were taken away in trucks in order that their clothing should also be treated. They did not return for many hours and when they did they had a hair-raising tale to tell.

They had been admitted to the de-lousing building, stripped of all their clothing and footwear. They assisted in hanging all this 'clobber' on rows of rails in a very large heating space. Large doors were closed and the de-lousing heating process began. The group of some seventy men, after showering, waited in a large room immediately outside the 'ovens'. During the first 'cooking' period and at an appropriate point in time, the German de-lousing operator came in to check that all was going well inside the oven but clearly, when he opened the first door, it was not. Flames leapt out with a roar and in not much more than a few moments the whole wooden building was ablaze. If there were spectators outside they were treated to the bizarre sight of a large body of completely naked and barefooted men fighting frenziedly to get out through doors and windows at top speed to gain sanctuary in the frozen snow!

Immediately and unexpectedly a substantial amount of shelter and many blankets had to be found. The absence of our friends was lengthened by the difficulty the Germans had in finding sufficient clothing for seventy men, including footwear, all of which must have come from captured British uniforms from the Blitzkrieg in 1940. Never a dull moment when one is a prisoner-of-war!

I had many turns round the compound with Frank Partridge who talked to me of Roman Catholicism, with Roland Beamont (post-war to become Chief Test Pilot of British Aerospace), Tom Lowry, Jimmy Pestridge (later of the BBC) and many others who, knowing that I had a repatriation ticket, were anxious I should write to their wives or folks at home when I returned. They were all identified in my notebook and numbered probably fifty addressees.

In mid-January news came that the exchange of prisoners was imminent. Sure enough, very shortly, a dozen prisoners gathered near the main gate ready for departure. The SBO wished me well and said that as I was the senior officer in the party (I had an automatic promotion to substantive Flight Lieutenant in mid-1944) he wished me to convey a message to the intelligence authorities as soon as I could: 'The Germans are assembling jet fighter aircraft at a location south-east of Belaria.' We had seen one of these aircraft flying low over the compound.

My friend Roland Beamont who had tramped the perimeter with me was the only other senior officer to see me off the premises.

Our party of twelve officers joined a hospital train at Sagan equipped with sleeping bunks throughout, plus guards with rifles. I cannot believe they imagined or expected the possibility of our attempting escape, but Germans will organise for anything!

I was close to the point of no return as far as POW life was concerned. An accumulation of thoughts about the existence in the Stalag would remain in my mind for a very long time and would be sifted out by my future life and remain as clear memories.

We called at other prison camp locations until the full complement of ex-prisoners had been gathered.

As I stretched out on my bunk in the train I wanted only to remember my feeling of thankfulness when I first walked through the gates of the Centre Compound at Sagan. I recalled the generosity of feeling for me by my companions. I had not eaten a meal for many weeks and showed physical signs that this was so. Extra pieces of bread and other items had been given me from their personal rations by my friends. I was very grateful.

Thoughts of the events and experience of twenty months from being shot down, trying to evade capture, St Gilles prison and prison camp life temporarily disappeared as I tried to get a grip on the fact that I was out of it all and was on my way home. I could not have be more relieved and thankful.

In the years that followed I came to know that prison camp life had taught me a great deal and equipped me with capabilities that I might never have gained elsewhere. I had come to know my room-mates very well and could anticipate their responses to all kinds of issues. Indeed the sifting of events that I refer to above helped me to deal with people in civilian life and took me way beyond the authority that comes automatically with a uniform. Strong personal views about anything soon had their sharp corners knocked off and we all gathered a maturity of greater quality than could be obtained elsewhere.

Our destination was Konstanz on the lake of that name at the German and Swiss frontiers. The route was circuitous and took us through Vienna over the Danube.

The guards on board were prepared to trade anything for cigarettes or chocolate. The purchases were varied and made with a view to collecting memorabilia. One officer bought a pack of erotic photographs, another tried to buy one guard's left jackboot and it took some time before the soldier-salesman eventually declined the offer – temptation was there but what could he do with only a right boot?

The journey had taken forty-eight hours when we finally arrived at Konstanz railway yard where the exchange was to take place – on the German side of the border. German youths lined the bridges over the railway as we walked to the Swiss trains. They spat at us, but fortunately their aim was poor. The Swiss Army had been partially mobilized to handle the international prisoner exchange and soldiers of all ages mounted the train when we passed into Swiss territory: they were from twenty years to greybeards of seventy. It was so good to see them and to be welcomed by the British Ambassador and his embassy staff as they passed through the train.

We persuaded one particularly beautiful girl to sit in our

compartment for a minute so that we could look at her and hear the voice of a woman!

The journey to the French frontier in Southern France was long and at the border we transferred into French railway stock. Here we were visited by an American Army Colonel in charge of the operation. He confessed that he had overlooked the need for locomotives for some time and when it came to the crunch had a problem finding a sufficient number. Apparently, too many trains had been shot up by Allied air forces! Soon after leaving the border we were given the most delicious food on compartmented trays; the white bread was heavenly. Two more special stops were made at selected stations to provide us with refreshment and general welfare before reaching Marseilles.

On the home front, at about this time, a telegram was despatched to Mary by the Air Ministry which said: 'I am commanded to inform you that 122719 Flight Lieutenant S.E. Harris crossed the frontier into Switzerland on 19 February 1945.'

The train came to a halt in the Marseilles dockyard. We lined up in threes and stood easy – but not for long. American medics came through the ranks with large cylindrical hand pumps, the conical ends of which were inserted in the front and back of our trousers, front and back of shirts and into armpits – we were de-loused! This having been completed, British and Commonwealth military boarded the Canadian troopship *Letitia*.

Action was immediate once we were on board. Clothing was taken away and replaced; showering and bathing began. What a wonder it was and what a relief to be away from the Third Reich. The food was good – EVERYTHING was good. Some found it vital to shower after every meal! We set sail with all lights and red crosses shining brightly, all the way to Liverpool – we were going home.

Unfortunately my notebook had not made the full journey; somehow it had gone missing. Amazingly I remembered every name and address and many of my friends' kinfolk replied, telling me of their joy at hearing news of their men first-hand.

The Mayor of Liverpool greeted us and a band played on the dockside. Here it was that I, among others, met Peter Churchill for an intelligence debriefing, and to whom I passed on the information about the jet assembly plant in Silesia, given to me by the Group Captain.

Homecoming.

Fourteen days later I stepped out of a train at Brighton, with another Brightonian POW, to be greeted by Mary. She argued with the policeman handling the taxi queue and got us to the front in quick time! In ten minutes I was back in my in-laws' house and met my small daughter, Catherine, for the first time. She was fifteen months old and I was a stranger; it was very confusing for us all.

I was physically free but mentally tied to imprisonment and to continuing thoughts of those who had helped me during my evasion. They remain deeply etched in my memory to this day.

CHAPTER 11

Home and News of Blindness

I had three weeks leave unaware of my next posting. During that time, Mary's mother cared for Catherine whilst we spent a few days in an hotel in Exeter. Our second daughter, Rosalind, was born nine months later!

The Allied invasion forces were within three months of complete success but the V2 rockets were still hitting south-east London. I went to Tatsfield to see my mother and father and wanted to take Mary and Catherine with me, but the wisdom of the home-fronters who had weathered the V1 campaign prevailed and I went there alone to stay a few days.

It was a good visit and another homecoming. The village folk came to see me and I visited them. I heard just two or three V2 explosions, the last of which was no closer than Lewisham in south east London.

My father and I walked up to 'The Grange', once the home of the Darwall-Smiths, and met Flying Officer Verney-Cave and his wife, later to become Earl and Countess Braye. I remember being shown some marvellous miniatures of their ancestors and talking a good deal about the war. He pointed out that I was a higher ranking officer (just!) and said he had never been able to get further than Flying Officer in the Administrative Branch. When he succeeded to the earldom they sold 'The Grange' to Donald and Melissa Maclean of the Burgess and Maclean spying duo.

After drinks with the Verney-Caves we took our leave and as we walked down the village green my father told me how he felt when I went missing for so long. He said my framed photograph helped him, but he had been much troubled throughout my absence by his memory of the day he accused me of being a thief. He remembered his threat to me to pay a visit to the police when I failed to give a penny change after buying a chimney cleaner.

'I was unreasonable and should never have said all those things. I'm sorry.'

'Stop worrying,' I said, 'You only know half the story anyway. It's time you knew what happened to the penny. In attempting to buy a Nestlé's chocolate bar from the station at Oxted I put the penny in the wrong machine and all I got was a brand new platform ticket.'

We stopped for a moment and together wept a little.

I learned that the first news the family had of me was when my first prisoner-of-war postcard was received at Tatsfield in November 1943, five months after I was posted missing. One more month and I would have been presumed killed in action. It was also made clear to me that Mary was the single force of optimism that kept the parents and in-laws away from acceptance of the worst.

I returned to Brighton and received news of my next posting. I was to go to RAF West Malling in Kent to a Rehabilitation Unit. Here I attended up-dating lectures and discourses on the views of others as to what we might expect when hostilities ceased. I remember one point from the latter: it propounded that there would be too many old people in the population by the year 2000. It seems to me they were right and I muse over the fact that I am one of them!

When we were given a demonstration by a helicopter which showed us that it was possible to fly backwards, I felt older at the sight of it!

I also had talks with officers whose job it was to find me suitable employment in the Royal Air Force. What would I like to do? I vouchsafed that as I had been teaching French in a prison camp perhaps it would be a good idea to do the same in the RAF Education Service.

'What a splendid idea,' declared the interviewing squadron leader. 'Go home now,' he added. 'You will hear from us very shortly.'

I returned to Brighton in an old Ford 10 car, ARK 110, which I bought in West Malling Village for £80 and drove home. I had never driven a car before, but I relied on my memory of the essentials of motor bike riding and made the journey quite comfortably. The car was in poor shape so we corrected all the faults; we then took a holiday in Herefordshire with Catherine to celebrate our new mobility.

I was posted to a job a long way from teaching in the Royal Air Force Education Service. I went to the Assistant Directorate of Organisation (Mails) at the Air Ministry and reported to Wing Commander R.E. Ridgway DSO, the Assistant Director at Ashley Gardens close to Westminster Cathedral. I had become a Staff Officer.

117

The department's job was to administer the network of postal units throughout Home and Overseas Commands and, as an interesting additional duty, to give answers to Members of Parliament when their constituents complained or needed information about the regularity of mails to and from themselves and their loved ones serving throughout the world. My guide and mentor at the department was Maurice Juniper Guymer, a Kingston-on-Thames solicitor serving as a Flight Lieutenant in administration.

To help me I was seconded, for a period, to Fighter Command at Bentley Priory and sat in with the officer responsible for mails distribution within the Command. I visited the Groups within the Command and had a splendid opportunity to study paper-work handling methods in the RAF. I was billeted in a large house in Stanmore and joined a family there; the lady of the house, although the wife of a serving officer, had spent periods away from home in internment, being of German extraction.

I visited some of the larger RAF Stations to inspect their treatment of mails, official and private and during my stay at Bentley Priory I talked with Douglas Bader and W.J. (Bill) Edrich *inter alia*.

The Assistant Director, Wing Commander Ridgway DSO and his deputy, Squadron Leader A.M. Gill DFC, were very reasonable men and I enjoyed being within the unit. I learned the art of good letter writing there, mainly from Maurice Guymer, particularly when it came to replying to an MP whose constituent complained that his son's letters were not getting through in good time. His remarks to his Member of Parliament, a very distinguished individual, were straightforward and colourful and I quote:

'I could get the letters from Malaya to England quicker by paddling a bloody canoe myself.'

I remember the name of the distinguished MP to whom this gem of a complaint was directed but I am close to a breach of the Official Secrets Act! Our investigation revealed that the airman in question was writing his letters home six at a time and dating them to indicate false intervals. I hope his father managed to keep the canoe and that his son had a good explanation.

I had joined the department in April 1945 and during the following year indicated that I would like to be granted a Permanent Commission. As a candidate I was acceptable and went forward quickly for a medical examination which included, as its last element, an eye examination. It was discovered that at the periphery of each retina there were noticeable signs of degeneration and failure. I was sent to the RAF Hospital at Halton and spent some time seeing distinguished eye specialists, who pronounced the condition to be incurable and disqualified me from holding a permanent commission. They pronouncd I would be blind by the time I was thirty-four – ten years later. The specialist opinion at Halton as to the cause of this condition laid the blame on the period of evasion and imprisonment in Bruxelles St Gilles when I experienced severe malnutrition. In their view this had triggered the problem. It was a bad blow. All I could think to do was to remain in the Service until my demobilisation turn came and I did my best to put it all into the back of my mind.

By now we had taken a small ground-floor apartment in Brighton just before Rosalind Ann was born in November 1945. Our decision was to remain there as it seemed to be the sensible thing to do in the light of what had become a different outlook on the future.

In early November 1946 the *Daily Sketch* reported that 'Flight Lieutenant Stewart Harris had taken Mme. Ninette Jeanty to lunch today.' She had come to my Air Ministry office, then located in Cadogan Gardens just 100 yards from the Peter Jones store. It was her first visit to London and she had found me by referring directly to Air Ministry Records Branch.

Her story reached the National Press the next day but I had it first-hand from her. I recounted what had happened to me from the very moment when I crawled into the roof-space at 'Donhead'. I heard that she had suspected that her neighbours might have given us away, but at that moment those responsible were not known. I told her that I felt entirely responsible for the whole affair, because if I had not decided to attempt an evasion nobody's life would have been lost or endangered.

Ninette's story was extraordinary, profoundly impressive and disturbing to me for at the end of it she told how her husband Paul had died in a concentration camp deep in East Germany.

Soon after the house was violated by the Gestapo she and her husband and son were taken to the Avenue Louise Gestapo Head-quarters in Brussels. Young Claude, the sixteen year-old son, was detained for some time but then released and for the rest of the war he went into hiding. She and her husband were tried by the German authorities, the offence being the harbouring of an English airman. Ninette Jeanty feigned madness and the court found, consistent with the law, that neither she nor her husband should suffer capital punishment when one of the accused marital partnership could be said to be insane. She was sent to a mental institution at Bonn and Paul went to a concentration camp where, close to the end of the war, he was shot in a massacre of prisoners by their German guards.

Months of incarceration with mad people finally drove Ninette to own up to the controlling medical authorities that she was not insane. The principal of the hospital, on hearing her confession, said that he had long suspected that she was not deranged. The war was then clearly in its concluding stages and he did not hesitate to extend hospitality and kindness in his own home where, for many happier hours, she taught his young family music and the piano.

I pressed her to tell me whether I could be of any help to her but without result. I was assured that she had friends to go to. I was to learn much later who these friends were. Claude had survived and was the recipient of his father's estate. Ninette was not a beneficiary and was then, at the time of our meeting, dressed as a representative of the Red Cross, the uniform being her total wardrobe: she was penniless. Clearly, friends must have been supporting her to enable her to come to England. Moreover, there were friends in London with whom she was able to stay.

In early December, my crew-mate friend, Roy Evans, came to see me at the Air Ministry offices at Cadogan Gardens to put a proposition to me. He had gone back to the Metropolitan Police soon after his return from Germany but had not stayed long; he turned to commissioned sales work in a variety of consumer goods but had found little success. Would I consider joining him to emigrate to South Africa where he felt there was a better future for young people with a need and urge to work. I said I would think about it and took the problem home where it was received with very mixed feelings. I felt that getting one's foot in a door could be easier and better paid in the younger and expanding economy in South Africa. Having been there in 1942 we had had an opportunity to size up our opposition in the populace.

Finally, after talking about it for some time we decided I should throw in my lot with Roy. He and I would try for a sea passage at once and called on all the shipping companies in the City of London up to Christmas Eve 1946. On that day we secured two tickets to South Africa each costing £50. There had been a block cancellation and it was not possible to contact replacement passengers over the Christmas period. Would we like two berths?

These £50 tickets to South Africa were sponsored by the South African Government headed by General Smuts. When his party lost the next General Election, the acceptance of immigrants by this method was abandoned by the new National Party Government.

In his autobiography *The Great Betrayal*, Ian Smith, the last Prime Minister of Rhodesia, declares he was told that this change of policy was judged by prominent members of the South African Nationalist Party to be a bad mistake. Their economy suffered thereafter from a shortage of thinking, potential executives from Western Europe.

After Christmas I requested an immediate release from the RAF and was out of the demobilisation centre in forty-eight hours.

This decision to leave our native shores unfortunately caused my family a degree of grief and dismay, but in early January Roy and I sailed for Cape Town on the Union Castle vessel RMS *Carnarvon Castle*. The die was cast for us but the whole venture was not undertaken lightly. There were, of course, some misgivings – I had chosen that my family should cut our home ties and face an unknown future.

CHAPTER 12

Emigration

We disembarked at Cape Town and found bed and breakfast accommodation for the first night or two, but fell out with the couple who took us in. They told us of the rate of charge for bed and breakfast when we first arrived, but the very next day the rate had gone up, so we quit their establishment. Pretty soon we took train to Durban where Roy's wife, Dorothy, had an aunt with whom we lodged for a short time, then moved into a small hotel where, unfortunately, the proprietor became awkward (I forget the reason) and at one point refused to release our passports which were in his safe.

We made industrial contacts and were invited by the Chief Engineer of one of the large British manufacturing subsidiaries in Durban to accompany him to the races in Pietermaritzberg. We had dinner with him and his wife the night before and discovered that she was having an affair with her violin teacher. The next morning when he picked us up he was accompanied by his very sexy secretary; the situation was complicated by his having a poor day with the course bookmakers and by the girl showing more signs of interest in us than in her boss! I won £18 on a horse called 'Blimey' and the result was so close there was nearly a riot amongst the unsuccessful punters! George VI and his Queen and daughters were touring at that time and only a few days before, whilst they were at the races in Cape Town, a riot took place over the disputed winner. I wrote home and told of my success and had a prompt reply from Mary questioning why I was enjoying myself and putting the point that it was no fun looking after two small children in ration-torn Britain. I had been so sure she would like all my news!

Roy and I decided to go on to Port Elizabeth as we felt the concentration of manufacturing industry there might offer more opportunities. I had contacted Canon Harold and Mrs Rolfe of Walmer (and late of Queenstown) to ask if we might stay with them. They met our train and were generous with their hospitality. Our search continued with Ford, General Motors, Dunlop, Mobbs Brothers, a shoe manufacturer, a wool trader, etc., etc. Finally, and successfully, we saw the Branch and Sales Managers of the Shell Company of South Africa in P.E. and secured the post of sales representative for Roy and a sales accounting post for me. The signals went back to the wives and we moved out of the Rectory at Walmer to an hotel in the centre of the town. The Rolfes had been very good to us and looking back I fear we were inadequately grateful. Mrs Rolfe was the Medical Officer for the Walmer local authority and was most helpful when recurrent attacks of asthma became troublesome. Roy had been baptised by our host and I became a godfather, an honour that still subsists.

In the parish within which our hotel was located we were fortunate to be befriended by the Vicar of St Cuthberts in Port Elizabeth, Canon T.B. Powell and his wife Laura whose hospitality was generous and whose cellar was replete.

Then family affairs began to develop: Roy's wife Dorothy and small son Richard came out first. It was not meant to be played that way, but our two daughters, Catherine and Rosalind, had unfortunately contracted whooping cough; for two small children (aged just over three years and one year respectively) this was a most distressing and debilitating period; Mary also suffered much anxiety and fatigue. When the girls recovered they all came out on RMS *Stirling Castle* six weeks later.

By this time I had secured a first floor flat in what had been the German Consul's house in Walmer and this was our base for our stay in South Africa. Mary got a job in a company selling baths and lavatories and we bought a car. We secured two native South African girls to help, one to keep house during the day and the other to take charge of our two small girls; they became good helpers. We hired a young man to bring the garden into shape but had to fire him fairly quickly as it was his intent to sleep during the day and to waken just before our return in the late afternoon! He was on hand, however, when a poisonous tree snake showed up in the garage and he successfully killed it as it came out of a length of drain-pipe. Three-year-old Catherine found another snake under a large stone and beat a hasty retreat. There were also many tortoises in the garden ranging in size from minute to those the size of tea-plates – they terrified Rosalind in all sizes!

Mary and I had to deal with another invader and fight off a bat which came nightly into our bedroom through the shutters; I eventually clobbered it with a tennis racquet!

Another irritation (especially for Mary) was the presence in the house of large spiders known as 'Berties'. She claimed they ran like racehorses and had gleaming green eyes! To this day she suffers from arachnophobia.

We worked and played hard; there was a tennis court in the garden and barbecues on the beach – but after a time serious problems arose: Mary developed a suspected tubercular shadow on her lung, my eyes began to rebel against the strong, clear sunlight and my asthma gave me severe trials. Unhappiness began to develop; apartheid bothered us both and when we heard from the house-agent that the German Consul wanted to repossess, enough was enough. We decided to return to UK.

Shell were good to us and signalled that they would recommend me to Shell UK. I had gained a good background in the accounting administration within a major distributing oil company and I had become proficient in the complicated field of petroleum stock holding and had acted as deputy cashier. This time was to serve me well throughout many future years in North West Europe and UK oil markets. Shell was an example of excellence in the conduct of a large company and I was fortunate to have such a beginning in international commerce; I was on my way, but I was not aware of it at the time.

We set about finding a passage home and secured berths on a Union Castle ship, the *Llanstephan Castle*, to Southampton via the East Coast route, through the Red Sea and Suez. Embarkation day arrived and a group of our friends came to see us off at the P.E. dockside. We were on our way home.

We very soon found that our cabin was little more than a large cupboard, with four bunks and no port-hole or air-conditioning. How could we possibly manage for six weeks of tropical heat, little room to move and two small children? We arranged with the Purser to disembark at Durban to seek another vessel taking the shorter West Coast route home, but at extra cost. We were fortunate and within two or three days of calling at the Union Castle office we went aboard RMS *Durban Castle* and found our cabin to be much more suitable.

After leaving Cape Town on the way home, we called at the island of Madeira for a few hours. We spent the time looking around Funchal, a delightful place, and armed ourselves with a good supply of bananas to take back; this fruit had been lacking in the UK since the beginning of the war.

After an incident free voyage we set foot on British soil on 5 June 1948, my brother Bob's wedding day, an event we were sad to miss. He married Evelyn and they had a family of three children, Christine, Tony and Gill. He entered Holy Orders early in married life and took up a curacy in Herne Bay, within the Canterbury Diocese.

We were met at Southampton by my mother-in-law and Mary's friend Brenda, who later became godmother to our yet to be conceived son, Stephen. There was much rejoicing at the return of the 'prodigals'.

CHAPTER 13

The Oil and Motor Manufacturing Industries

Mary's parents welcomed us back to their home in Brighton once more. Immediate contact with Shell-Mex House in London revealed that they had no advice of my coming. However, they later replied to say that they would entertain my joining, but would I wait six months for a vacancy to occur? This I accepted and shortly afterwards volunteered to run my father's shop in Tatsfield to enable him and my mother to take a holiday. Mary and I moved in with them and trusting to my luck rather than my judgment they quit for two weeks and flew out to Montreux. These two weeks tested my memory of how to cut up and bone a side of bacon, weigh and pack butter and use a bacon slicing machine. When they returned we went back to Brighton and I promptly got a job with the Danish Bacon Company as a sales representative in the city of Bedford and its environs.

In this position within a wholesale grocery company I sold the full range of groceries and provisions and every part of a pig's anatomy, salted, smoked or pickled in brine in barrels. The only uplifting incident involved my participation in a scene in a butcher's shop in Kempston in Bedfordshire, when a lady customer had an epileptic fit. She began to topple but I grabbed her in time and helped her to a seat. The butcher and I loosened her blouse at the neck and stood by with a drink of water when the attack was over. I then took her home and returned to the shop to report that all was now well. The butcher, who had hitherto been unco-operative and off-hand with me, immediately gave me an order for a barrel of chitterlings (pig intestines), a high value item which bumped up my commission very satisfactorily for that week. It was quite a victory and the only barrel of pigs' innards I ever sold in my life!

I did not enjoy the job but was glad of some income. I lodged in a tiny back street of Bedford, travelling back and forth at weekends via the Birch Bus Company to Kings Cross, across London by Underground to Victoria and thence to Brighton and then a reciprocal course on Sunday evenings.

I prayed regularly for the day when Shell would offer me a job. They were as good as their word and came up with a post at Tunbridge Wells in the Lubricants Department, which I accepted.

As I was about to leave the Bedford scene, one of my customers, Bill Brinklow of the Brinklows Bakery chain of shops, offered me a job in his organisation, but the oil industry beckoned and I began to travel daily from Brighton by train to Tunbridge Wells.

Stephen was born during this period in June 1949. On my first visit to the nursing home the Matron was anxious to show me the baby and happened to be holding a red-headed child in her arms.

'Where is he?' said I, thinking that the parents of the red-head must be lucky.

'This is he, you chump!'

Mary was not well after Stephen's arrival, in spite of a fairly quick and easy birth. When she felt fit enough we returned to Tatsfield to stay with my parents and I bought a 250 cc motor-bike to get to the office at Tunbridge Wells.

This move signalled the start of a campaign to obtain council housing for ourselves in an area where I was well-known. The effort began with a renewal of contact with my old friend John Ferguson of Oxted, whose son's funeral I had attended for the Royal Air Force in 1942. He was a Councillor on the Godstone Rural District local authority and eventually was instrumental in getting us a new council house at Limpsfield Chart, from whence I continued to travel to the office at Tunbridge Wells in all weathers through the lanes of Kent, past Penshurst Place, on that awful motor-bike!

The Branch Manager, McLeod by name, recommended me as a Shell Sales Representative candidate and I attended Shell-Mex House for an interview board. There then occurred a Christmas Party at the Spa Hotel in Tunbridge Wells where Mary met the Shell-Mex & BP General Manager, Haygarth by name. She used the opportunity to say how fitting she thought I was for the sales posting. However, when the results of the board were announced it was said that I was completely unsuitable!

Telling me of the result McLeod said: 'Whatever went wrong, Harris?'

'I have absolutely no idea, Sir.'

Moreover, at that time I did not know or suspect there was a reason. Before long, however, it seemed certain that Haygarth had intervened. Maybe he disapproved of Mary's responses on and off the dance-floor. I was to meet him again several years later and he remembered me well enough. Soon after the Spa Hotel event I was transferred to a small distributing depot at Redhill to a simple product-distribution clerical job. The vengeance was complete!

I began to think of fresh pastures and quickly obtained interviews with the London Personnel Managers of Esso and of Regent Oil Company. I made no impression on the Esso man, but I did learn that in those days Esso did not sent telegrams but essograms! A fruitless visit and quite useless information!

The Head Office of Regent Oil Company referred me to the London Manager of Regent, George Limmer. George was a toughie and knew his business completely; I was fortunate to find him on a good day and, as a result, was confirmed in an appointment as a Sales Representative in the London South Division at Wandsworth. Suddenly things were improving: at last I had a reasonable salary and after a short on-the-job training period I took charge of a fairly productive territory in South East London.

The war-time non-branded pool motor fuels were still being sold. If one was lucky one persuaded a garage proprietor to display the Regent advertising globe on a forecourt pump or pumps. The next move was to persuade him to buy pool petrol from Regent. This was more difficult but one made some sales and headway.

The south-eastern postal districts were my 'patch' and I began to make friends who, over the years, would serve me well. The saying 'have a smile for everyone on your way up or they will have none for you on your way down' began to pay off. As a new man on the area I did not lose a single customer and gained others. Little did I know it at the time but I was laying down a network of contacts for the future.

I became interested in local government politics and joined the Liberal Party, supporting candidates standing for seats on the local authority. When it became time for new elections to my ward I was persuaded to stand, but I had little hope of success as a Liberal. There were five candidates for three seats and I canvassed hard. The result was extraordinary: I came top of the poll, beating the Chairman of the Council into third place! I was jubilant and enjoyed the congratulations of my hard-working supporters.

The fortunes of the Liberal Party were at such a low ebb that I was contacted by Liberal HQ and asked if I would agree to be the parliamentary candidate for Petersfield in Hampshire. I called George Limmer at Regent's London Branch and sought his advice and permission; his answer was in the negative in forthright terms which stirred me to realise on which side my bread was buttered. Therefore I refused the Liberal nomination and later found that my job made great demands on me, causing me to give up the local government seat after a period of two years.

In early 1952 I had a call from Ninette Jeanty; we had exchanged Christmas cards since our last meeting at the Air Ministry in late 1946. We had lunch at the National Liberal Club where, shortly before, I had been made a present of membership by a distinguished ex-Stoke-on-Trent Mayor as a reward for my winning the local government seat. I showed Ninette the smoking room where no women were allowed, but where Mrs Eleanor Roosevelt had entered 'by accident'.

'Could I please be allowed to enter accidentally?' asked Ninette.

'No, please not. I'll never be forgiven – and I'm such a new member too!'

Certainly things had changed for her since we last met. There were real prospects of her being offered a job in the European post-war Control Commission in the Belgian team. She had written a book about her life after arrest by the Gestapo and had some prospect of appearances on television and in radio programmes. When she said that she was finding it difficult to reach all her contacts and friends I offered help. After all, I had a job and knew my way around.

So I fitted in trips to the BBC Lime Grove Studios at Shepherds Bush, TV producers at Alexandra Palace and radio programme makers at Broadcasting House *inter alia*. I went with Ninette to friends, amongst whom were Dame Sybil Thorndike and a retired Headmaster of Harrow, whose name escapes me but with whom we had dinner. As the association went on it became easier to talk and I recall asking her whether she had any knowledge of Petrofina, the Belgian international flagship oil group. At that time it did not seem to me to be a particularly significant item of conversation.

She was in the habit of calling me at home and there came a time when I said: 'Good morning. What is on today?'

'I will not be meeting you today. I am calling to tell you that my English friends have advised me that I would be unwise to continue our association. They have persuaded me that you may only be helping me because you see in it a way to advance your position in the oil industry.'

'Your friends are quite wrong. Surely the help I have given you is sufficient proof of my goodwill.'

'We do not think so.'

'Then there can be no further point in our continuing to meet – and I am sorry that it is so.'

Further correspondence petered out and time went by until I saw in the newspapers that Ninette was to marry Canon Charles Raven, a very wealthy, erudite and well-known Cambridge theologian. The marriage took place at St Martin's-in-the-Fields Church in London. The reception was in the crypt and I sneaked in but gained no sight of them. They lived in Cambridge and some years later, when I was in that city on a business assignment, I called in the hope I might see her. I saw the Canon who knew of me, but Ninette was not there. It was my last attempt to re-establish a connection.

Her book was published in 1948. In a heavy international anti-communist atmosphere she had some difficulty finding a publisher and it had been necessary to go to Dublin to get a printer. The book tells in its early pages of the preparedness of the Jeanty household to offer a 'safe' house to help fleeing Communists from the German Occupation régime. It has a foreword written in August 1947 by Dame Sybil Thorndike, who was a well-known Communist sympathiser.

I believe that Ninette Jeanty's rejection of me had more to do with the fact that, in my travels to help her, I had begun to gain too close a knowledge of an intellectual circle of Communist sympathisers in the UK. One has to bear in mind that McCarthyism was very much alive in this general period and I had overheard conversations in which very bitter references to Senator McCarthy were made.

Mme. Jeanty featured in radio and television programmes and was one of Eamonn Andrews' victims in 'This is your life'.

Within a year the Government and the oil industry announced that the pooling of oil fuels would end and companies would distribute their own branded gasoline and derv fuels. This fundamental change away from the war-time pool arrangements was to signal the onset of sustained competition between the oil companies. It was to be the harbinger of a transformation in the relationship between the oil companies and the service station network throughout the British Isles. Within months the companies secured exclusive representation on all service stations and large sums of money were made available for operators to refurbish their facilities. The oil companies themselves bought land and developed new service station outlets to lease or to be managed by their own staff.

At an early stage of this market change I was asked to join the Regent Oil Company's London Branch Manager's personal staff to lead a small section to deal with the new situation. It was my task to assess, write up and present deals to the Head Office, to instruct lawyers and follow through with them to legal completion. These propositions came in from the market-place in Greater London and the Home Counties.

At this time I handled many of the deals negotiated with the National Car Parks Company headed by Donald Gosling and Eric Hobson, his partner. Both are now multi-millionaires and the former was knighted by Harold Wilson in his Prime Minister's Retirement List. The giant NCP Car Park group started in London with the financial help of the London Branch of the Regent Oil Company.

Forty years or so later I was received by Hobson in his London headquarters when I called on behalf of St Dunstans, the charity for the war-blinded. I failed to secure a donation.

Within months I was further promoted to the Head Office of Regent Oil on the staff of the General Sales Manager (GSM) to handle the flow of business from the branch in London and the Southern Branch at Brighton. I enjoyed the job, particularly for its gift of many opportunities to make up my own mind about financial propositions and to recommend accordingly.

The GSM was an American named Oscar Fish from the Texas Oil Corporation. The Regent Oil Company had been sold into the joint ownership of the Texas and Chevron corporations when it became obvious that the financial demands of the new regime in the UK market-place called for immense financial resources.

In my job as one of the three aides of the new GSM I was not able to develop a personal liking for Oscar. Equally, I do not believe he was over-fond of me, but the job was done and done well for the London and Southern Branches. They gained from the swift financial decisions and approvals they received through my office but Oscar did not take an appreciative view when the Southern Branch Manager asked if I could go to Brighton to a promotion post. Oscar said: 'I don't like you bright guys. I'll tell you with no bullshit that if you have any ideas about moving on, I will make sure that you go back into the field at its lowest sales point.'

That seemed pretty clear to me and at the first opportunity I walked out of our building and into the tiny office of the newly-arrived French national oil company, Total, in Aldwych, London and told my story. Within a week I received an offer and began working in Bush House where the staff was made up of a General Manager, Charles Redman, a French lady named Routy from Paris, a secretary and myself.

Within a short time it became apparent that my first special task was to begin the preparation of a five-year plan and forecast covering the entry of Total into the UK petroleum market. To prepare me for this job and to acquaint me with the structure and policies of the parent company, Compagnie Français des Pétroles, I went to their Head Office off Boulevard Haussmann in Paris for three months. I enjoyed every minute and covered, on foot at weekends, most of the sights and monuments of that wonderful city. I even tackled a risqué show at a theatre in the Rue Caumartin, where I was able to follow the jokes and the dialogue – which like the dresses, did not amount to much! My French was improving apace.

I returned home, interviewed and hired sales staff and briefed them on their conduct of a market-intelligence survey.

By this time I was fortunate in having made friends with my colleagues in Paris, one of whom came to London to advise me in the preparation of the five year forecast and report. He was an ex-cavalry officer whose company I enjoyed in both London and Paris, but sadly he died not too long after I left the Company. The report was well-received and was followed by Mary's and my first trip on a tanker, the *Astrolabe*, out of the Thames to the refinery at Donges near Nantes in North West France. I well remember one of the meals aboard the ship – it was the Captain's favourite dish: pig's trotters. I think both Mary and I had difficulty in swallowing our food! An interesting but short trip in the owner's suite.

The five-year growth plan had been accepted in principle and Total began immediately to move into a fully structured selling mode. It was interesting and exciting and throughout I carried Charles Redman whose contribution was entirely wrapped up in his interpretation of and efforts to become a figurehead of distinction! So when the time came for the developed staff structure of the company to be agreed, I had high expectations of a good appointment in the plan. But I was disappointed. I did not think of it at the time but it became clear to me afterwards that whilst the assignment had been successful, my personal style had not reached a point consistent with senior office. I had to thank Charles Redman's opinion on my social standing for that.

I decided to leave when I had an offer which I just could not refuse.

This came from the Managing Director of Dodge Brothers, the UK offshoot of the Chrysler Corporation, to be his Personal Assistant at the Kew Gardens plant which was the UK assembly point of Dodge trucks and Simca motor cars. This job was to entail moving into a variety of posts within the factory where I held the leadership position but retained my appointment as personal assistant to the MD.

I had now served thirteen years in the oil industry and was about to spend four years in a very different industrial atmosphere.

The Managing Director, Wendell Clough, was an ex-US naval officer and a charmer. His wife Frances was a delightful member of the Firestone Tyre family. I was assigned immediately to aid Fred Clem, the Supply and Material Control Director, and with him I learned how the Motor Industry made progress in spite of itself. Fred was, in my opinion, an unpleasant, uncouth bully. He was ill with some sort of spinal problem and was soon to leave me to the wolves when he went into hospital. The departments of the company just did not adequately co-operate with one another and each department head, whether he was a Director or Manager of Accounts, Engineering, Inspection, Production, Sales, Service or Spare Parts, had a personal stock of long back-stabbing knives.

The packing of knocked-down kits for export was also my responsibility and my greatest bane. My most difficult customer/enemy was a Mr Meswani of Premier Motors of Bombay, an assembly plant owned by Chrysler International. I performed for one year in this role and left it when Fred Clem returned from extended sick leave.

I spent a further year as the Managing Director's troubleshooter, one year as Head of the Economic Studies Department and one year as Southern UK and Northern Ireland Sales Manager for trucks and cars. The period with Chrysler began in 1960 and ended, thankfully, in 1964. But I had become wiser in the process.

In Fred Clem's Supply Department I had to learn fast the intricacies of the buying and scheduling into the factory of every kind of material and manufactured parts which made up a heavy goods vehicle's chassis. Seventeen to twenty of these complex units moved down the production line each day, mostly of differing specifications. Additionally I had the responsibility for the department packing and shipping for export. Many large crates of sets of parts for assembly into heavy vehicle chassis went overseas to customers whose business it was to assemble and sell the company's vehicles.

Personal Assistant to the Managing Director meant plant trouble-shooter, persuader, peacemaker or senior leader in an emergency situation. A troubleshooter in an automotive assembly plant does not win friends, but has to influence people. As I have said, we made progress in spite of ourselves. The whole company cried out for tough industrial leadership which, unfortunately, Wendell Clough did not possess. He was too nice a guy and he was replaced.

One event I shall always remember. I spent a long weekend in Monte Carlo at the Grand Prix as the guest of Rubery Owen Ltd., a very large automotive engineering concern and our sole supplier of truck chassis frames. Sir Alfred Owen was the chairman and the driving spirit behind the British motor racing fraternity in the shape of the BRM racing car and was our host.

Stirling Moss won that year and I spoke with him and others of that vintage and skill. That weekend was a memorable high point.

I also cherish one other event during my Chrysler days. It involved me and my colleague, the Northern Sales Manager. We were ordered by the Board to proceed to Birmingham, to visit one of the Company's more important customers in an attempt to try to mend and restore to normality the relationship between the parties which was currently at a low ebb. A serious dispute had arisen as a result of an error by the Company.

We arrived outside the great man's door, knocked and a strong voice shouted: 'You'd better come in!'

I opened the door and Ken, my friend and colleague, dropped to his knees and moved, in that position, a fair distance across the carpet to the customer at his desk. He then lifted his hands as in prayer saying: 'We are heartily sorry for these our misdoings.'

The charged atmosphere evaporated and all three of us collapsed in laughter and the problem was over.

'They were bound to send you two buggers. No-one else would have been able to persuade me,' was the closing remark as we departed.

Midway through my fourth year with Chrysler, Mary and I had a home visit from the Isherwood family of Eccles – Arnold and Mary Isherwood (the Chairman and his wife) and Albert and Mair Cook (son-in-law and daughter) whom I had come to know during my time with Total Oil. They owned and ran an oil products distribution company called VIP Petroleum. Their headquarters was in Eccles, with branches in London, Wolverhampton, the port of Barry in Glamorgan and Newcastle. The purpose of the visit was to invite me to go to Manchester as the Company's General Manager at an enhanced salary. It was a good offer from a company which had made its name as an independent operator. I liked the idea very much – it was attractive to me but I was concerned with a special point: did they contemplate selling out to any bidder, now or in the future? The answer was firmly negative.

However, there was strong objection from Mary; she appreciated the need to seek advancement but was not attracted one iota by the prospect of living in or near Manchester. Moreover, Catherine, our elder daughter, had a pleasant job at the National Gallery; she had not long recovered from a road accident outside St Bartholomew's Hospital where she was on a State Registered Nurse (SRN) course. The result of the accident ruled her out medically for further SRN training. Rosalind had not long left school and Stephen was midway through his education. What to do was the issue within the family – I did not feel good about it, but we did need the extra salary. We had come up from zero not too long since and had very little capital savings. It seemed as good an opportunity for advancement as I was likely to get, and I knew the oil industry and the outfit well. I did not find working for Chrysler and the motor industry a very enjoyable experience and the opportunity to return to the oil business was very attractive and tempting.

After much heart-searching I accepted the job and my appointment appeared in the *Financial Times* prematurely. As a result I then found myself not only in trouble at home but embarrassed at the plant at Kew Gardens. In retrospect I probably deserved it, but the change did bring about considerable and welcome financial growth. However, it was accompanied with more than a fair share of anguish for the whole family.

I went to Manchester but Mary would have nothing to do with the choice of a new house. Before leaving our Surrey home I visited the National Gallery to express regret that Catherine would be leaving and to Stephen's school at Wallington for the same reason. Ros left her job and we eventually moved into a good detached house in Sale and tried to settle down.

At this time I was also aware of the fact that my field of vision was noticeably reduced. In 1945 I had been told that I would be blind within ten years but now, in the early 1960s, I still had some forward vision. I was being examined at regular intervals by ophthalmic specialists in the War Pensions Department of the Social Services Ministry. These examinations were carried out by a Manchester specialist who had so far reduced the time that he took over the investigation of my eye condition that my bottom barely touched the chair he provided! I wondered how many men he examined in one day at this rate and concluded that someone ought to know that they were not getting his full attention, so I reported my dissatisfaction.

The new appointment with VIP Petroleum was not easy in one main area: the Chairman, Arnold Isherwood, quickly proved to be a tough, unreasonable character. I had dealt with him during my time at Total Oil when it was necessary to negotiate a new agreement or a revision of prices for the petroleum products supplied to his company. His toughness was that of a bully but when a change of that mood happened it was a delightful experience and one could do no less than like him but he had never recognised tact or diplomacy. I had been appointed General Manager and later became a Director and still found no relief from his infuriating attitude in all things.

One of his favourite expressions was: 'The trouble with you young buggers is that you don't realise I am halfway back from a problem before you've even thought of it!'

At forty-two years of age at that time I did not take kindly to such comment, but when I reached the equal of Arnold's age much later on I realised he had a point.

Albert Cook, his son-in-law, whom I succeeded as General Manager, had a long exposure to his father-in-law and found it more than enough. He came into his office less and less as the time went by. Eventually he invited me to move into his room and to take over completely. I am happy that he, Albert, a very likeable man, has long been free of his problems of those days and has led a life of great public service to this day. I feel a great respect for him.

A personal assistant joined me, a young man who had been invalided out of the Royal Green Jackets, having been partially deafened by a gunshot. Bruce Petter was of the Isherwood family group, his maternal grandmother being Arnold Isherwood's sister. Bruce was born into the Petter engineering family and his father, Kenneth, had been a Rolls-Royce aero-engineer and a member of Mountbatten's staff in Washington DC during World War 2. Bruce's uncle, Teddy Petter, had been the designer of the long-serving RAF Canberra aircraft and the Gnat fighter. He, Teddy, also had played a vital part in curing longitudinal instability in enhanced speed Spitfire derivatives when serving at Westland Aircraft Manufacturers. I enjoyed Kenneth Petter's company very much and discussed with him whether it was he who had come to Skellingthorpe when we had trouble with superchargers and Stromberg carburettors, but it was not so.

Our three children had, as I said, come north with us: Catherine and Rosalind were appointed to the Secretarial Department and as a goodwill representative respectively and Stephen became a pupil at Chetham's School in Central Manchester.

Mary and I felt, in due course, that it was time for a holiday and we took a cruise on the Canadian Pacific Liner *Empress of England*, visiting a number of exotic locations and enjoying a well-earned rest. On our return at Liverpool Docks we were greeted by Catherine and Bruce who were clearly there to tell us of a new development: they announced that they wanted to marry!

Wedding preparations were soon in full swing but other events back at the office were quick to follow. Albert Cook advised me of the family's intent to negotiate the sale of the company to an American outfit called Signal Oil & Gas of Los Angeles. This company was active in North Sea exploration and had a growing network of trading subsidiaries in North West Europe and had its headquarters in the Neuilly area of Paris. I was invited to take part in the final signing ceremony and was, upon its conclusion, appointed a director.

The new ownership insisted that the company had to operate under a revised product-pricing and financing régime; this necessitated regular visits by me to the Paris headquarters. During these visits I was asked to take part in the establishment of a new automotive fuels marketing company for Signal in Brussels; this new subsidiary would bear the VIP brand name and would be conducted overall from my office in Manchester. Signal had chosen the local manager and would I take the matter forward and do all that was necessary to found, direct and manage the effort?

Accordingly, the first task was to register the new Belgian company. In order to do this we had to attend at a special Belgian advocate's office in Brussels and, in following legal requirements in these matters, we had to set before the law officer a sum in cash exactly matching the foundation capital of the company. Thus Signal's treasurer and I had to carry a suitcase on a flight from Paris containing 1,000,000 Belgian franc notes through Brussels and place it under the nose of the lawyer. The papers had then to be completed with all that money lying around. We were relieved to get back to the company's offices in Paris at the end of the day and deposit the cash in the safe. We certainly needed a strong drink to relieve the stress!

The treasurer, an American, and I celebrated the day's work at dinner in his apartment in Paris in the evening. When it came to bottle-opening time he said:

'Do you like the wine?'

'Thank you, yes – it's very good.'

'Can you tell me what it is?'

'Yes, I think so. It's a Burgundy.'

'How the hell can you tell that? You Europeans really know your wines!'

I did not answer the question. It would have been a pity to tell him I had seen the shape of the bottle!

Staff had to be engaged for the new Belgian company, an office found and prospective customers visited. I interviewed all the staff candidates and confirmed that they should be engaged. I told each successful member that I would be having a drinks party later that evening at my hotel and would be glad if they would come to launch the new ship. At the party I was approached by one of the new sales staff who said that he was ashamed of his performance earlier in the day.

'Why so?' I said.

'I am ashamed that you had to interview me in French. It is bad not to be able to speak the language of the interviewer and for an Englishman to be speaking French to me is just too much!'

So much for the reputation of Englishmen at that time! It is very different now.

Before Catherine was married I was despatched on a mission by Claude Geismar, the European director of Signal. I was to visit and inspect a business at Enschede near the frontier of the Netherlands and Germany and to negotiate with its owner as to whether he would sell his business to Signal. During my time there I took a telephone call from Mary, who by sheer inspired intuition, worked out where I might be. The message was:

'Please come home. Thieves have broken into the house!'

My driver and I set off across the Netherlands to Schiphol Airport at high speed all the way. Fortunately the flight time-table was in my favour and I took off almost immediately. I arrived at Heathrow to find that the last flight to Manchester was about to close. When I told my story, the airline held the flight but staff had lost my bag. There was a delay until it was found and I was rushed to the aircraft.

The reception from the other passengers was frosty and hostile as it was late and the last service of the day. As I sat down heavily in an exhausted condition I was greeted by my neighbour with the words:

'So you are the bugger we've been waiting for!'

'Yes,' I said. 'Do you want to make something of it?'

I explained what had happened and he immediately ordered a large Scotch for me!

We were robbed of many things, but they caught the men within forty-eight hours. Dressed in the same decorators overalls they tried to break into another house in the neighbourhood and were apprehended. It was a short career in crime for them.

Arrangements for the marriage were nearing completion at the time and there were many wedding gift items in the house. Fortunately none of these were taken, but Stephen had made ready for his sister's big day by buying a new shirt and he was most upset at its disappearance! The robbery could not have been more badly timed.

During the travelling between Manchester and Paris on one Friday afternoon I walked into the departure area at Orly Airport to find a mass of officers from the UK Armed Forces surrounding the bar, none of whom were below the rank of Air Commodore, Brigadier or

Commodore. In the midst of this crowd with his back to the bar was an Air Vice-Marshal: it was Mickey Martin whom I had not seen since 1942 at RAF Wigsley on the Lancaster Conversion Unit. He recognised me and we had a very short and entertaining session with everyone else gathered around. I had not seen so much scrambled-egg (gold braid on caps) in one location before that meeting! Mickey and I talked on the phone occasionally thereafter and as a gesture of goodwill to a famous airman, I authorised that he should have his car fuel tank filled at the nearest VIP station to his home – as a 'one-off' expression of my company's regard.

A most important change was soon made to the petroleum supply policy involving the company's imports from the Rotterdam international market. We were accustomed to buy all our needs from brokers on our own account but now had to accept an imposed régime: the parent company, Signal, deliberately priced products to shift profits from VIP in England to the Signal trading company in Paris. In the trade this system of pricing is based on the 'High of Platts' published price at the time of shipment, plus insurance and freight. Platts is the market price indicator published daily and is expressed in high and low prices for the day. Our price would become the High of Platts plus insurance and freight charges from Rotterdam – CIF (Cost Insurance Freight). This was to be the price level deemed appropriate to take out the profit from the UK subsidiary (our company in Manchester) in sufficient quantity to favour the parent and keep the subsidiary at a break-even position. I warned that the price was much too high to suit our trading position in the UK and it was certain that it would put the company into substantial loss. We ran a year and produced a loss of £1,000,000. The accountant had reached this result and had teleprinted this figure to Paris without consulting Arnold Isherwood – still chairman – or myself. We were both telephoned angrily from Paris with the question: 'What the hell is going on?'

An air of crisis hit both the Paris and the Eccles offices and within forty-eight hours we were invaded by a team of accountants to look at the books. Claude Geismar, the European head man for Signal (later to be a senior negotiator for Armand Hammer of Occidental Petroleum) came over and told me I would have to go. I told him I would not agree, for I had warned of this situation in advance. He threatened me with a court case and I said I would welcome such a move. I heard no more of that, but soon was lumbered with the permanent lugubrious presence of an American accountant from Los Angeles after our own accountant was fired.

I suddenly became persona non grata with Arnold Isherwood, who later took Catherine and Bruce aside and told them they should give their support to him if they knew on which side their bread was buttered. They should speak to me and tell me I was being unreasonable and should go. They told him they would have nothing to do with such a proposal.

I had already complained to Geismar that I was being thwarted in my development of reforms by the Chairman. I declared to Geismar that it must surely be bad policy to retain the Chairman of a company which has been taken over. His reply was that Arnold Isherwood was the cross I had to bear.

A special aide was assigned to me who, but a short time previously, had been the Chief Executive of BP in Italy and now, with Signal, had a roving commission amongst subsidiaries in the European group. He was a smooth operator, an excellent linguist but quite out of touch, especially at the level in the market in which VIP operated. He had a lady friend who sent him telegrams which landed on my desk and usually ended 'de ton panier de fruits délicieux' (from your basket of delicious fruit).

On one occasion I waited on a bench at Manchester Piccadilly Station for the arrival of this aide. He had chosen to come in on one train and was leaving on the next one back to London. His purpose was to bear a threatening message to me from Paris which told of the direst of outcomes if I did not resign. His journey was fruitless.

A change of tactics soon came. I was offered a job in Paris as Marketing Co-ordinator for the whole of the Signal group in Europe. The salary offer was very good and I undertook to go to France and spend a period there and work myself into the job before moving house to Paris. I had the feeling that the offer was a sort of placatory gesture with a sting in the tail. It would take an epigrammatic form in due time.

I took up residence in a charming leased apartment in Neuilly and went home for a weekend each fortnight. Eventually the crunch came: I was presented with a new contract of employment, one of the clauses of which said that I would be available to go to any part of the world WITHOUT NOTICE. We argued about it for some time and one weekend at home, after talking over a new idea with Mary, we took a decision. I would not return to Paris and I wanted six months pay to quit entirely; they accepted and they paid.

CHAPTER 14

Trident

If a man does not keep pace with his companions perhaps it is because he hears a different drummer; let him step to the music he hears, however measured or far away. (Thoreau: Valden VIII)

We sold the Manchester house quite quickly and went to live temporarily, once more, with Mary's parents, who were then in retirement in Sussex. Catherine and Bruce had come south previously and lived at Merstham in Surrey. Rosalind had become a stewardess with British European Airways and Stephen had finished his schooling. He obtained a temporary job on a local industrial complex; he assembled back-pack weed-killer equipment for export. We were about to make a fresh start.

I was anxious for our plan to succeed, for it was clear that I ought not to delay such a new course at forty-six years of age. The loss of my field of vision had become very advanced by this time and in this context, as well, there was no time to lose. What has also to be said is that I had a supportive wife who was perfectly capable of providing the necessary brains and commercial background we would need in future – I could not have done without her.

I regret never seeing Arnold Isherwood again. I am glad that contact with Albert and Mair Cook was restored when they came south to the marriage of Catherine's daughter, our oldest grandchild, Victoria. It was so much later, but very welcome. Toria and her husband, Michael, have provided us with our first great-grandchild, Harry, two years old and he now has a baby sister, Eleanor.

The new direction plans all began in 1966. Over a number of years previously I had become very disenchanted with working for other people. The seed began to germinate when Shell moved me out to the depot at Redhill and the feeling gained strength when I worked as aide to Oscar Fish at Regent Oil Company. When the crisis came to a head in Manchester I felt that it marked a point where a decision to work for myself had to be taken. My situation was comparable to a play in Rugby football when one shouts 'Mark' as a high ball is caught and, momentarily, the game stops before a deliberate new directional kick is taken.

Up to the time of the take-over of VIP Petroleum (Isherwoods) by Signal Oil & Gas, a proportion of the company's petroleum product supply requirement was bought from Tampimex Oil Products, a successful oil-broking firm based in London and an associate company of the Ingram Corporation of the US. I knew the senior executives of the company and remembered that their Managing Director, Manfred Schubert, had asked Albert Cook and me whether we would consider becoming totally supplied by Tampimex at all VIP's storage points in the UK. This could, he said, be mutually very attractive but Albert was not interested.

I decided that with the ideas I had for setting up as an independent distributor in Southern England, Manfred Schubert was the man to see. Mary and I had six months pay in our pockets from Signal and a further £15,000 available from our house sale in Manchester to set up such a company. We were prepared to take a gamble.

So one day I set off to London from Sussex and Mary telephoned Schubert ahead to say I was on my way to see him with a proposition which he might find interesting – a tiny bit of theatre, but it worked. The visit produced an agreement in principle that a distribution company should be formed and that I should return with a detailed proposal including a sales volume and cash flow forecast, plus ideas as to a likely Thameside ocean bulk storage depot.

We went to work on the plans assuming that the capital base of £15,000 would be provided by us. We produced a market assessment for the proposed area of distribution in London and the Southern Home Counties and a cash flow chart showing how expenditure and revenue would develop over the first five years of operation. Our bulk petrol (gasoline), diesel, gas oil and kerosene storage point was to be established at the newly-built Dutch-owned Van Ommeren public storage terminal on the Thames at West Thurrock in Essex. I worked on the assumption that my estimates would be achieved plus or minus 10 per cent. This was not a Harris yardstick but stemmed from a remark made to me by Etienne Dalemont, one of two most senior directors of the Compagnie Français des Pétroles in Paris – half-owned by the State at that time. He said, 'Stewart, if you can achieve better than plus or minus 10 per cent of your forecasts you will have done very well!'

DAILY EXPRESS

High octane Trident

ROY MACKIE
TALKING MONEY
85 LONDON WALL
EC2M 7AD
01.588 7311

SETTING up in competition against the multi-national oil leviathans with £5,000 and 45 years behind you may seem a very short cut to the bankruptcy court.

So indeed thought the friendly advisers of Stuart Harris when, aged 45, he decided to do just that in 1967.

Undeterred by such gypsy warnings he went ahead, called his company **Trident**, roped in the family, bought a couple of tankers, and rented some storage space at Purfleet, then arranged for the first tanker full from Europe . . . and went looking for some customers.

Bustling

"I had some second thoughts at that stage," the one-time Lancaster bomber pilot admits.

His only thoughts now are for expanding Trident—which is expected to sell a massive 19 million gallons of Trident petrol this year through his 200-odd filling station customers.

Based in the growing commercial centre of Croydon, Trident is now a bustling oil company employing 75 people and with 22 tankers on the road.

The Harris team have taken on the big guns of the business by cutting prices on its imported petrol, and providing fast and personal service.

After a small first year loss profits have grown to an expected £45,000 this year.

From the petrol base 50-year-old Mr. Harris has taken Trident into lubrication oil and central heating supply business.

"We cover the whole of the Home Counties and I think we have pretty nearly reached the limit as far as filling stations go—the development of the business will be more and more from the other side," he explains.

Behind him in the venture are his wife Mary, a co-director and son Stephen, at 22 a hard working rep for Trident. Daughter Rosalind is another one of the family team.

Eventually a stock market quote is a possibility, so the public may get a chance to back the man who, when most are thinking of comfortable middle age, decided it was time for independence.

145

THE TIMES   TUESDAY AUGUST 15 1967

Oil cargo arrives from Germany

A new independent petrol company, Trident Petroleum, reports the arrival in this country of its first tanker load of refined crude from west Germany. Mr. Stewart Harris, head of the new company, said yesterday that, in spite of the current delays over supplies to Europe and the United Kingdom there had been no difficulty in obtaining supplies and a further 1,000 tons load of refined crude was expected shortly.

Within the next three weeks the company will have 10 stations operating in Kent, Surrey and East London and will offer motorists petrol at prices ranging from 5s. 1½d. to 5s. 5½d. —the same prices as those offered by Jet Petroleum, the major United Kingdom independent.

He knew his business.

Mary and I returned to Tampimex and agreement was reached on all our proposals. We suggested the name 'Trident' as the brand name of our products and the name of the company would be registered as Trident Petroleum (London) Limited. The name was suggested to Mary and me by the trident in the hand of Britannia on the reverse of the penny coin, still extant in 1966.

One major change to our plan was agreed: Tampimex proposed that they should put up the £15,000 capital in the form of £5,000 as the share capital and £10,000 as a debenture. Thus our own funds would remain intact. We also agreed that the share-holding should be 51% for the Harrises and 49% for Tampimex. We were asked to claim that Trident was a Harris venture and that Tampimex was the supplier only. We entered into an agreement confirming that exclusive supply position. Tampimex were concerned that their other major oil company clients in the UK should not learn of this venture. I did not like the prospect of having to deny the truth, but had little choice other than to live with it.

The first person to contact me to ask whether it was I who was registering a company called Trident was the editor of the *Petroleum Times*, who had noticed the registration and found the share capital of £5,000 to be unusual and worthy of investigation.

I was happy with this single enquiry, although I felt that provided I entered the market quietly I could make progress. I estimated I would not have to face any serious competition for three years; in those days the companies did not move quickly and, sure enough, that is exactly what happened.

With the plans well under way we moved to a new house in Croydon and set up in a small first floor office in the town centre. At this time my father became my accountant and was a great general advisory help in that field. We had come together when I first told him of our plans and I had never felt closer to him; at last I felt he trusted my judgement and I valued his advice. The first heavy blow of this period came when he died suddenly. I missed him more than I had ever felt possible up to then.

Just before this setback, the Chairman of Ultramar UK, already making its own difficult beginnings in the UK, offered to buy me out if I would drop my idea and join the Ultramar UK board of directors. He tried hard with all sorts of flattery and entertainments, (including the Mirabelle for dinner) but I turned him down. Tampimex also made it quite clear that they were not in favour.

At this time also, the building of the Van Ommeren terminal at West Thurrock ran into serious difficulties: the major tanks had begun to subside because of faulty foundation work. Their prospective customers had deserted elsewhere; I was the only client left and, at the beginning of my operations, leased all the smaller storage space they had in the shape of ten small tanks to hold my petroleum stocks: their foundations were sound.

As our first shipment from a West German refiner was discharged into those tanks, I stood alone on the dockside and watched the hoses throbbing as the cargo was pumped ashore. The coaster-tanker had come in from Rotterdam and discharged 1,000 tons of gasoline (petrol) and gasoil/diesel fuel. It was a chastening moment: I had an office, two road-tankers and drivers standing by, three sales representatives, daughter Rosalind and Mary as office staff, son

Trident tanker on Westminster Bridge.

Stephen, with van, standing by as a service station converter and petrol pump painter, plus a four motor car fleet – but no customers! It was a scenario that demanded action and determination. It seemed to me at that moment it had been a long road since 1929 when I first explored the shop premises at Tatsfield – and I had just ninety days to pay for this newly acquired cargo!

In the meantime, my Cargo Inspector went quietly about his business, jointly supervising the discharge of the cargo with the ocean terminal management. This activity, despite the bulk of the different products, is a precise job; it involves the specific gravities of the products and the temperatures, both at the loading and discharge installations. All this data has to be converted finally into accurate measurement of the cargo in volume terms and converted into tonnages at 15 degrees centigrade.

In the lead up to this critical point I had discussions with HM Customs & Excise on the issues and responsibilities of importing hydrocarbons into the United Kingdom and the payment of Excise Duty and Value Added Tax thereon.

The Ministry of Energy, as it then was, also appraised me of my duties under the regulations concerning Trident's responsibility to hold stocks of hydrocarbons in support of the national strategic stockpile policy.

But there had been more interesting decisions to take: the design of the company's logo and public advertising signs was determined with the help of a small but very talented design group headed by John Button of Button Associates who did all the original graphics, the printing of the trading documents plus the livery of all company road-tankers. It was very exciting conceptional stuff!

The process of selection and appointment of our sales representatives and truck drivers was completed at the most propitious moment, having regard to the arrival of the products and the signing up of customers. It all went according to our plan: we went out to meet the motor fuels retailer market, many members of whom we already knew, armed with a strategy and tactics to suit the market condition.

I resolved that we would agree deals and take decisions more rapidly than did other companies. I believed that I had a three-year 'honeymoon' period before my main competitors really woke up and ganged up against my presence!

In an attempt to mask my intentions I ordered that for the first three weeks of our sales operation we should do no more than talk to prospective retailer customers, both to judge what response we would get as a newcomer and to give the opposition's sales staff an opportunity to feed on whatever they could. Their reports on what they thought we were up to would reach their managements in due time! Accordingly, hair-raising tales came back through the trade grape-vine telling of our generous trading terms. Clearly we had stimulated some confusion among the giants and lesser corporate pigeons in the Southern England loft of the oil industry! I knew that sales representatives have active imaginations and they passed back their ideas of market intelligence to their employers. They did what we thought they would do and painted a picture of exaggerations. We went quietly about our business after turning over a harvest of market information.

On 7, 8 and 9 June I elected to try and further the Trident cause by spending the three days in and around Fleet Street. I saw all the broadsheets of the day where I was most courteously received by those responsible for energy affairs.

I had read the reports in the *Financial Times* by the Energy Editor, Christopher Tugendhat, and during my work with Total Oil I had become aware of him and of the directorship that his father, Dr Tugendhat, held within the Manchester Oil Refinery. So, when I called at the *FT* Headquarters I asked for Christopher T. I was seen almost immediately by him – a great charmer – and I was introduced to Arthur Sandles, the Editor of *Men and Matters* at the time, and I was his leader in the daily feature in the next issue.

The *Daily Telegraph* man kept me waiting a long time, so I eventually sent a message up to him to say enough was enough, but in March 1968 Richard Walker gave me quite the best feature, with an apology that he had kept me waiting the previous year. The feature showed a picture of Mary, our daughter Rosalind, son Stephen and myself.

The Times came up with short pieces on a number of occasions later on, as did others, including the Institute of Directors, of which I had become a member.

The Financial Editor of the *Express* did a feature much later and I recall his reporter asking me whether I minded their saying that I had been a pilot of a Lancaster rather than a navigator; it would please Max Aitken, the owner, so much more!

We made a modest loss at the end of 1967, secured our 50th outlet at Oxted in Surrey in June 1968, broke even at the end of that year and thereafter moved into profit where we stayed until 1973.

This was the most exciting period of our lives. The business grew steadily and the volume of sales moved into tens of thousands of tons. Larger storage tanks were leased and the number of the road-tanker fleet moved steadily into the twenties. Our transport office at Grays in Essex was always under pressure to give service. Our staff at Croydon grew in one of the new high rise office buildings there. Trident Lubricants were launched. We ventured into road tanker general haulage through ELM Haulage Limited (Mary's initials) and began to lease garage forecourts and operate them through a subsidiary called, not inappropriately, Neptune Service Stations.

Annual Trident motor rallies and the London Schools Football Association were sponsored. It was a privilege to stimulate the schoolboy game in London and a thrill to watch one of their Cup Finals at Arsenal's Highbury Stadium from a seat in the Directors' box.

I was invited to serve the new Petroleum Industry Training Board as Chairman of their Medium & Small Companies Training Committee. Many new acquaintanceships were made and I was author of various industry texts (of doubtful quality, I fear) in the trade magazines *et al*. I even recorded an interview at the BBC for the 'Today' radio programme, but it did not reach the air, being dubbed as 'not sufficiently catastrophic'.

However, life was not all a bed of roses, for the operation of a distributing organisation often gives birth to the unexpected. A problem arose one winter's afternoon late in 1969. I took a telephone call from our Transport Manager and learned that our newest tanker had been involved in a fire on the premises of a small customer in Bognor Regis. Both vehicle and premises had been damaged.

The Bognor police were asking for a senior member of the company to attend as soon as possible. I decided to go myself and set out at once with my driver. An Inspector of Police greeted me on arrival and as his narrative unfolded some ghastly breaches in basic gasoline delivery procedures were revealed, both on the part of our driver and of the operator of the garage.

According to the report given, on the arrival of our tanker the driver exchanged pleasantries with the customer during which it was accepted that there was plenty of space in the underground storage tank. Neither the quantities in that tank nor those in the compartment of our vehicle were checked by driver and garage owner, contrary to the strictest of rules. Delivery began and both the customer and the driver repaired to the office for a cup of tea. Unfortunately, the underground tank could not accommodate the quantity in the tanker's compartment; consequently petrol overflowed and began to run into the garage workshop. Here another hazard awaited: contrary to proper industrial safety rules, our customer had allowed an open electric fire in the workshop and it was not long before an explosion took place. Two or three cars were sprinkled with burning débris and flames destroyed the aluminium entrance door which lay in metal droplets on the concrete threshold.

The fire service had been called after the explosion and the fire-engine arrived in very short order. It was driven by a fireman who had a financial half-share in the business which, no doubt, helped to quicken the passage of the fire engine to the site! The hose from the road tanker delivering petrol was still connected and petrol was still overflowing out of the underground tank onto the forecourt. This situation attracted the attention of the driver of the fire-engine. In his consternation and zeal he drew his axe from his belt and in one hefty blow severed the hose thus causing the fuel to flow even faster and setting fire to the tyres of the tanker!

An unknown person bravely halted a worsening scenario by turning off the tap on the vehicle! I understood that our driver was taking shelter round a corner a little way down the road and could be seen peeping out from time to time!

At the conclusion of the Police Inspector's report, I summoned a spare vehicle from our base at West Thurrock. We waited till midnight when the police closed the centre of Bognor as, in convoy, we towed the fire-damaged vehicle to a central car-park and discharged its remaining cargo into the reserve vehicle.

Our company was issued with a warning and both driver and Trident customer were taken to court and fined.

The customer claimed that the fire had destroyed £500 worth of National Insurance stamps; remarkably, the police, the National Insurance authorities and his insurance company failed to believe him!

At the end of that night I uttered, through clenched teeth, those immortal words of King George V: 'Bugger Bognor.'

I took a very serious view of the incident and had shown this by attending myself. We were given a warning not to allow driver breaches of regulation again. I was particularly upset at the severe damage caused to a beautiful brand-new tanker.

CHAPTER 15

The Manor House

In 1972 we bought the Manor House at Blechingley in Surrey.
At that time we lived in a house in Sanderstead, a little south of
Central Croydon, but had begun to look elsewhere, including adverts
in *Country Life*. Mary spotted a property on the first page in the
advertisement section and we went to have a look. For both of us it
was love at first sight: a beautiful Caroline house rebuilt in 1643 and
classed as a Star Grade 2 Listed Building. There were 28 rooms, three
acres of gardens and 22 acres of grazing land on lease to a local
farmer. A double garage with a flat over and a shell-lined grotto made
up the total picture.

The then owners were anxious to sell. The family company had
collapsed and they had to part with the property. It was offered at
£65,000 and we bought it at that figure. Without knowing the future
we could not have guessed how important it would become to us
over the years.

We had earlier sold a house in Mermaid Street, Rye, which had
been the company's property for the entertainment of customers;
now that furniture was very conveniently to be used at the Manor
House – and Trident made a useful capital profit.

To have bought a house of such proportions would have been
absurd for just two people and certainly 'over the top', but we had
some other ideas. Our two widowed mothers were living in a house in
Sanderstead, together with Mary's Aunt Edith, a sweet, unassuming
lady. The mothers found the upkeep of the house and garden
somewhat burdensome and it seemed a good idea that they should
sell up and live in our spacious accommodation.

My mother, Gracie, eventually decided she would go over to Kent
where my brother Bob and his family lived, but, sadly, she died before
the removal was arranged. Mary's mother (known in the family both
as Peg and Dolly) and her sister Edith duly moved to the Manor
House and settled down. There was sufficient room for them to have
a separate kitchen, bathroom, sitting-room and bedrooms and to be

Manor House (frontage).

quite independent, but without the anxieties they had previously known.

Rosalind had, by this time, married Rolando, who was Spanish and whose mother and brothers lived in Las Palmas. They made the accommodation over the garage block into a comfortable home and Rolando joined Trident.

The Manor House had an interesting history, particularly in the closing twenty-five years of the eighteenth century and the early years of the next. It was owned by a Mrs Hughes-Ball, a widow whose ne'er-do-well son fancied the high life. Toward the close of the century a certain Admiral of the White, Sir Edward Hughes, came on to the domestic scene and married Widow Hughes-Ball. He had done well personally at sea in the Navy and had taken many French prize-ships in the Indian Ocean within the period of the Napoleonic Wars. He was rich and added considerably to the fabric of the Manor House, including a small personal retreat in the garden, under which he constructed a grotto with tiny sea-shells covering the ceiling and walls. This small building had been extended by a twentieth century owner to provide a double garage, plus accommodation.

I wrote to the Ministry of Defence to find out more about the

Admiral and shortly after took a phone call from a lady archivist, who was delighted that anyone should ask such questions about Sir Edward. She sent me a cut-out detailing his life and career from the National Biography. Today we keep a framed colour photograph of the Admiral's portrait which hangs at Greenwich Naval College.

Following the death of Sir Edward and Lady Hughes, the spendthrift son inherited the Admiral Hughes prize fortune. He became known as 'Golden Ball' and seriously took up with high life and the leading ballet dancer of the day, Maria Mercandotti – the Margot Fonteyn of the period. They both died in poverty in France around 1810.

It may round-off this historical look-back at the Manor House if I mention that there was a 'presence' in the building. I was keenly aware of it but had never been susceptible to the metaphysical before. The foot of the flight of stairs up to the rooms once meant for the servants, was its haunt. The air there was especially cold but with a pleasant, strong perfume which lingered. I lived with the presence until I began to look for a position to hang a ceremonial sword, once the property of a male member of my maternal grandmother's family. This man was an officer in the Volunteer Forces at the end of the nineteenth century. In a house with such a peaceful atmosphere I failed to find a home for it and sold it at a local auctioneers. Soon after that act I discovered that the presence upstairs was no longer there.

The most generally known and best-liked gentleman of Blechingley was Uvedale Lambert. Some time after we arrived in the village we invited him and his wife to dinner. Conversation on that occasion revealed that Canon Charles Raven (now married to Ninette Jeanty), had been Vicar of Blechingley. The Lamberts were quite astounded when we recounted our connection with Charles Raven and his name continues to crop up in our lives.

I write this story at my home in Hampshire and I am taken to Holy Communion at St James the Less Church in a tiny hamlet nearby, where a friend, Hamilton Lloyd, is Vicar. He knew Charles Raven and one of my Royal Air Force friends, Denis Street (one of the fifty officers shot after escaping from Stalag Luft 3). Hamilton and Denis had both learned to become pilots at the same flying school in the United States.

The long arm of coincidence once again.

Author in garden of Manor House.

Early in 1973 it became evident to Mary and to me that I had run out of steam, having gone non-stop for a number of years. We decided that I should do a round trip on one of the Union Castle ships still running a service round the Cape of Good Hope. I left in early March and returned five weeks later. I travelled first class and really relaxed, met and liked a lot of new friends on the ship and renewed contact with friends we had made when we lived in Port Elizabeth, particularly Laura Powell, the widow of Canon 'TB' Powell of St Cuthbert's. I had not been to the wine producing area before and now when I drink Stellenbosch wine it revives a host of memories.

During my absence Mary headed and ran Trident (which by then had 50+ employees) as if it was something she had always done! Some time before my departure I had bought a Rolls Royce, adding it to the company's fleet, and was taken to Southampton Docks in it. Mary bade me goodbye and returned to the car to find that an idiot tipper-truck driver had collided with it for no good reason. When I returned five weeks later the repairs had still not been completed!

I came back to a troubled atmosphere in the oil industry in Europe.

At the first of our resumed meetings with Tampimex we were told of serious petroleum price rises coming through later in the year; we also learned of the threatening behaviour of OPEC (Organisation of Petroleum Exporting Countries) which was especially militant in its proposals to nationalise all oil production operations within its member states. The UK's automotive fuel prices were controlled at the pumps by Government order, the Callaghan Labour Government being in power.

The months of April to July passed with the company continuing to make good monthly net profits, but the crunch came in August. The OPEC countries nationalised all foreign oil producing activities and more than doubled the price of a barrel of crude oil. Immediately all our independent sources of supply doubled their export prices and, as a result, we were in deep, almost instant trouble, as the retail prices at the service stations remained controlled. We had many taut and bad-tempered meetings with the directors of Tampimex. They agreed to ask the French state-owned company, Elf, to examine Trident with a view to there being a sale and takeover. All concurred that the matter was urgent and a delegation came from Paris very quickly. They liked the outfit, but they did not have products in sufficient quantity to supply us. We needed 65,000 metric tonnes per annum to serve our 205 service station customers and to keep going. They turned us down, but the head man said:

'Monsieur Harris, vous avez bien formé votre société. Nous pouvons la regarder comme une serre avec toutes les informations en vue.' (Mr Harris, you have a very well-formed company. We can look at it as if it were a greenhouse with everything in view – or something like that.)

However, the answer was still: 'Je regrette mais non.' (I am sorry, but no.)

I asked Tom Hutton, the Managing Director of Total Oil (the other French company), if he could look at us quickly as a purchase proposition, for we were having to sell our products at half the price we were having to pay for it. He agreed and was enthusiastic in a most friendly way. We went through a similar examination and all the Total top brass went over to Paris to sell the deal to the parent board. Tom came back almost in tears. The answer was the same and for the same reason. They had not and were unlikely to be able to obtain the additional 65,000 tonnes needed to keep the Trident company going. A new refinery supply point they had at Flushing in the Netherlands would not come on stream in time to help the Harris cause.

At this point and after further talks with Manfred Schubert and John Cairns, the Financial Director of Tampimex, it was agreed, under pressure from Mary and me, that we would continue to be supplied by Tampimex and that the two participants, Tampimex and the Harrises, would share the losses; with a view to the future, we would foresee the sale of Trident when the UK market came back to orderliness and profit. This plan was overshadowed by risk but sheer international financial necessity suggested that it should not be too long before government, or the players in the international oil industry, would perform a collective rescue act. Our understanding with Tampimex lasted around two weeks.

Two things happened. The first is conjecture. I believe that Schubert as Managing Director of Tampimex was compelled by the parent company, the Ingram Corporation, to renege on our understanding. It is my opinion that John Cairns set the fuse for Schubert with his parent company's Board. Cairns was not a man to take risks. He exuded a lack of genuine enthusiasm for our cause.

Secondly, Tom Hutton, Managing Director of Total Oil, in a further attempt to help me, had sold me two or three cargoes of gas oil/derv out of their Immingham refinery to keep us going and for which I had paid cash. Cairns became aware of this and on the following day telephoned our bank to tell them that, as our major supplier, all support from his company was immediately withdrawn. Despite a high daily cash inflow and a six-figure bank balance the bank pulled the plug by freezing our account. In an immediate gesture of sympathy the manager arranged a luncheon for us the following week.

In the midst of the international oil crisis all the press and the public were greatly sympathetic, giving birth to a letter of thanks from me in *The Times*. Both Mary and I felt that we had been pole-axed. We went for liquidation at once and I chaired the creditors' meeting three weeks later. The Transport and General Workers Union steward for the Grays/West Thurrock area was the only man to strike an offensively discordant note and I felt I was chairing a committee arranging a funeral. The meeting appointed Robson Rhodes, the accountants for Tampimex, as liquidators. It is my opinion they demonstrated typical methods and manners of liquidation in the exercise of which they took particular pleasure.

After the meeting the Trident party adjourned to an adjacent pub to refuel and recharge morale levels.

Jim Barker, our solicitor from Manchester vouchsafed to me that: 'Every good business man has at least one liquidation under his belt.' I was neither receptive nor convinced.

We had fought hard for the whole length of Trident's life and even had to remonstrate *en route* with such bodies as the BBC and the *Evening Standard*, a London daily. The former had portrayed a nefarious oil company called Trident Petroleum in its daily radio 'soap' about 'Mogul' a fictitious oil group which never did anything underhand and never made a mistake. It was a simple case of defamation. The *Standard* used our name similarly in a strip cartoon featuring James Bond. They published an apology. But it was all over bar the shouting.

However, I did have a sympathy call from one of the best-known liquidators in the business, Sir Kenneth Cork of Cork Gully, when he said:

'All very sad and all the result of this crisis.'

We had started with capital funds of £15,000 and the eventual outcome of the liquidator's work produced a sum just short of £500,000 which meant that everyone got his money back at a cost of the liquidator's fee of 5 per cent of each debt. Mary and I had no job and a pile of a house to maintain. There were some ex-Trident service stations that I had to avoid passing for fear of disgracing myself emotionally. We had run a happy company efficiently and profitably. Events outside our control had stepped into play and wrecked it all.

In his obituary of Trident on the City page of the *Daily Telegraph* on 31 August 1973, Roland Gribben said: 'Trident Petroleum, the biggest of the remaining cut-price petrol retailers, yesterday became the latest and so far most important casualty of the increasing squeeze on the independent operators.

'Industry estimates show that it has about 0.2% of the total United Kingdom petrol market and 0.5% of the market in the South East...'

But what to do next? We had lunch again with Alan Candelot, the Bank Manager, who promised his bank's support to the pair of us. The Manor House was to be our guarantor, for property values were on the way up.

Three months after the meeting of the creditors the Government lifted price controls on automotive fuels at the service station pumps.

Our agreement to share the losses with our partners until the market corrected itself would have precisely fitted this development. It is difficult not to look back in anger on those who were so short-sighted and lacking in visceral fortitude.

I was now fifty-one years old, practically blind and had somewhat overrun the forecast of the specialists in 1945 when they pronounced that I would be sightless by the age of thirty-four. And now, following the asphyxiation of Trident, I could hardly be considered a good candidate for any prospective employer.

CHAPTER 16

Company Doctor and Adviser

The Bank Manager would not tell us the words used by our erstwhile partners which caused him to freeze our accounts, but he conveyed to us that we had his confidence and the support of the Midland Bank. Our mortgage debt was £45,000 and all we had was my blind disability pension. He foresaw the growth in property values and, I believe, was aware that we would not let grass grow under our feet. We went home slightly bloodied but unbowed.

Within a few days Mary and I returned to our offices in Croydon to recover a few personal items. The office was unlocked, with nobody in attendance, and two oil paintings, the property of the company, were missing from their positions. I was concerned that with the office in an unsecured state they might have been stolen. However, this was not the case and the liquidators responded quickly, the two pictures re-appeared and I felt I had won a small, satisfying moral, if ephemeral, victory.

It is my opinion and experience that liquidators are bullies and evidently can lack care and respect for the property to be handled by them. My view of the accountancy profession had never been high and it was to settle at a new lower level before the liquidation was complete. The accountancy profession, which is reactive and deals only with the history of pro-active movement of money, seems to me to assume unacceptable levels of arrogance when they sense they have a little more power than usual. There quickly came a time when I resolved to personally deal no longer with Robson Rhodes and asked Trident's auditor, Roger Lugg of Roger Lugg & Company, to be helpful and fight my corner for me. It was ironical but I must say he did well and fought some telling skirmishes successfully. I was tired of being threatened and treated disdainfully.

One of the facts of life at that time was the overdraft that kept rising inexorably; at its highest it reached £59,000. The other troublesome issue was that my disability pension barely covered our living expenses. I felt we could only run a short period within this scenario as interest rates were climbing. Early in 1974, I began a job-searching effort and secured a number of interviews by direct approaches to companies or by responding to their advertisements for senior staff. I saw H. Brammer & Co., P & O's oil offshoot, Rank, Everest Double-Glazing, by invitation from the Chairman and many others. I was nearly fifty-two years old and handicapped: it was not the best time in my life to attract invitations to a senior industrial appointment. Mary and I had to use our own resources.

I began to put my resilience to the test and felt that the Manor House had to be used. It was good-looking both outside and in. How could it be done? We eventually came upon the idea of offering it as a venue for very stylish business conferences. I started to make a list of prestige companies, which I had obtained from Chambers of Commerce registers, including the United States Chamber in the UK. At the time I felt that this effort could well be fruitful. I asked my brother's daughter, an Honours graduate in Graphics, to do some magazine advertisements and a modest brochure. We secured a good catering firm and the campaign began. The Manor House facilities were good: the library was well furnished, the dining room seated twenty people, the kitchen and scullery were large and the garden a delight.

I had developed a strong mailing list but the responses did not exactly fire us with confidence. For some six months or so we averaged only 1.5 seminars a week. The combination of a modest profit margin and indifferent prospects made me decide to stop the effort and conserve our strength and our resources.

There was one other idea worth developing: we put in an application to the Godstone Rural District Council to open a first-class restaurant. We knew of a fully qualified and experienced chef who was prepared to join us – provided we bought him a Larousse cook-book, which we did forthwith!

At the same time, I contacted the headquarters of the British Helicopter Association, located in Redhill nearby, and discovered they were short of landing pads. I asked the local Council to consider granting permission for a helicopter pad in our garden, where the lawn would provide plenty of space for such a service.

When the applications were publicly advertised the local press, true to journalistic form, forecast in an article with a heavy black headline that the skies over Blechingley in general and the Manor House in particular '...would be blackened with helicopters'. Two events followed: my friend, Uvedale Lambert, called to tell me of his opposition to the plan and the Planning Office of Godstone RDC wrote to tell me that our application was refused. The police authorities felt that patrons of our proposed restaurant would cause a traffic hazard when entering and leaving the main gate, despite our being in a reasonable two carriage-way country road.

I gave up the idea. No helipad marred our lawn and the blackening of skies over our part of Surrey was averted! The British Helicopter Association and our prospective chef were disappointed, as were we. But we had to go forward somehow. One door shuts ... so another one shuts!

I resumed hard work on the development of the mailing list and began to get assignments from UK and overseas companies for personnel recruitment and general consultancy work. The latter included, for example, attracting the interest of offshore oil prospecting companies in the UK to onshore oil licences available for sale. These licences were held by European and Canadian energy groups and were located on mainland Britain. I was even asked to attempt to set up sales discussions with major oil companies for licensed areas in the Mediterranean, including western offshore Italy, Sicily and Sardinia. One European licence-holder had a senior Dutch geologist whose nose had been put out of joint by my being asked to help by his chief. He was utterly shattered when I found interested parties and confessed that he did not like me, but admired the degree of success I had achieved!

Other opportunities arose to solve local difficulties for companies which had ticklish personnel problems. In one case I was asked to visit a distribution company by its Chairman and Managing Director; he said that his company had reached a good level of activity but seemed unable to move on. Would I visit and make a report? I spent a month with the company during which the problem became clear: two men had started the company, the Chairman and the Sales Director. Quite evidently the latter was a source of difficulty. He knew everything and credited others with very little ability. He was strongly over-assertive and ungrateful to boot. Morale was very badly affected throughout the unit. I reported to the Chairman after thirty days to that effect.

'Thank you, I know all that. Will you deal with him for me? He is my friend and I feel that if you step in for me it will become clear to him that whilst things must change, our friendship will be unaltered. Can you operate on that basis?'

I replied: 'Of course and I will do my best.'

The Sales Director took it all very calmly and with good grace. The situation was saved and a friendship confirmed.

The work was producing an income but still not enough to stem the rate of interest on our borrowings. With the double failure of our plans for the Manor House still in our minds, I contacted our agricultural tenant and told him that I would be seeking a rental increase for the land on lease to him. His reply came quickly in the shape of an offer to buy. Pretty soon our bank overdraft displayed a substantial reduction and I was comforted by this development.

During this somewhat uncertain period I replied to a letter in the *Daily Telegraph* from Max Hastings. He told of his intention to write a book on Bomber Command and appealed for ex-members of certain Groups and Squadrons to write to him. He came down to the Manor House where we spent three hours talking about my experiences and many features of life in the Command with which he intended to deal. It was an interesting visit.

The most intriguing and disturbing question sought from me was whether I knew or had ever heard of a camp in the North of England holding two thousand ex-Royal Air Force aircrew judged to be lacking moral fibre (LMF). I did know of one officer and two NCO cases whilst with 50 Squadron, but knew nothing of a camp for such people and of such magnitude.

I was able to say that there had been a centre for miscreant and/or high-spirited young aircrew officers at Brighton, with a Wing Commander (ex Warrant Officer) as Commanding Officer. He was alleged to greet new entrants to the unit by the spoken gem: 'I got your papers 'ere wot don't look too good.'

I had been a Fellow of the Institute of Petroleum since 1966 and had become a committee member of the London Branch. In 1978 I became Chairman of the branch in the capital and had begun to move again in senior circles of the oil industry.

I recall about that time I was asked to sit on a quiz panel at an international oil seminar. Several weeks later I received £50's worth of Harrods gift vouchers, which I promptly spent as part payment for a new suit. Things were looking up a bit – every little helped!

In my consultancy work I had met Peter Ellis Jones, then the Secretary/Chief Executive of one of the independent operators in the North Sea. He also had a connection with the Swiss Avia Organisation, the largest independent distributor group in Europe, based in Zurich. Peter asked me if I would accompany him on a visit to Avia headquarters, to meet the officers of the organisation and to discuss with them their possible entry into the UK oil distribution scene. I agreed and in early 1978 took up the post of Chief Executive of Avia (UK) Limited based at the Manor House. My task was to recruit privately owned oil distributing companies to Avia. This meant they would re-brand the products they sold and the whole of their operation would carry the Avia logo.

I recall two incidents during my first visit to Avia. I met a man who spoke both German and Romansh, the Latin based language still spoken in the east of Switzerland. The second recollection is being asked a key question by Hanspeter Osterwalder, the Avia International President:

'What will be our most difficult task in making this attempt?'

I replied:

'To overcome the Anglo-Saxon's lack of final confidence in any cooperative effort of an international nature.'

This answer always comes to the surface of my thoughts when I hear the national argument about the European Monetary Union. The difficulty is rooted in our national psyche. To think of it brings on a very strong feeling of frustration, for I am a convinced European.

So I went to work for Avia and eventually recruited five privately owned companies. I enjoyed the Avia task and the counsel of my new Swiss friends and UK colleagues.

The appointment with Avia lasted for three years and the five member companies were retained up to the time I decided to quit. There was no issue left within the company that the members themselves could not solve – including particularly the matter of the final act of complete involvement in the Avia International system. Moreover, I found that in industry circles I was too closely identified with Avia and, accordingly, the core of my independence as a consultant was becoming eroded.

So the departure came about and one evening at the Grosvenor Hotel in London I was entertained to dinner by the Avia heirarchy; as a parting gift I was handed a large Swiss cow-bell complete with leather collar bearing an inscription on a small brass plate. As I did not intend to get into the cattle business its use would be somewhat limited! Maybe it has some purer significance of which I am ignorant. The memory of my kindly Swiss friends would have been quite enough – but it was a different, happy gesture.

About this time I was elected to the Council of the Institute of Petroleum, an appointment I held for six years. The Institute is the representative body of the UK Oil Industry embracing standards of performance in production, manufacturing and distribution. Its standards of production and analysis are in wide use throughout the world and it has many of its individual members working worldwide.

Three months later I was invited by the Chairman of a manufacturing company to meet with a view to examining whether or not I would join an associate company within his group engaged in petroleum distribution. This man was known to me and I immediately recalled a clash we had when his subsidiary's sales people were trying to poach Trident stations when I said:

'For every Trident station you take from me I will personally take two of your outlets.'

It seemed to do the trick at that time and he had some memory of the incident and of my prickly response.

My friend sought a Managing Director, being greatly pre-occupied himself with his other business interests. I lunched with him and we came to an agreement that I should take up the appointment.

I went home with the news and as an immediate result we decided to put the Manor House up for sale. It was no longer in our sole possession for we had sold the double garage block for £22,000 and had divided the main house into two dwellings, selling the more recent section, added by Admiral Hughes at the turn of the eighteenth and nineteenth centuries, for £34,000. So we were out of the financial wood. The next permanent stop would be a house in another location.

Our removal took place on a bitterly cold, snowy day. The countryside looked beautiful with a lovely white mantle, but roads were treacherous. We arranged to store our furniture and spent the removal night in an hotel; it was too late to contemplate a journey by then. Next day, with a loaded car, including dog, we left for

Hampshire to stay with daughter Catherine and son-in-law Bruce until we found a suitable house.

I joined the new company in January 1982 and two or three weeks passed before I assumed the role of Managing Director. It was time enough to think about the owner and the company and observe and talk to the staff. I was fairly 'hyped-up' by the time I took over.

The company was operating in a low state of morale: the retail service station market was in competitive turmoil and the customers were very unhappy. A director and other senior sales staff were refusing to take telephone calls, money was pouring out unnecessarily in the fight to hold business; some senior male staff were returning daily from liquid lunches quite incapable of working efficiently. The staff knew very well that things were not going well.

My first instruction was to the receptionist telephone operator.

'I want to know the name of the first person to refuse to take a telephone call – especially if the caller is a customer or one of our sales representatives – with immediate effect.'

It was a certainty that everyone would know of this instruction within seconds.

Next I ordered that we should toughen up our competitive stance with our customers and special terms were to be finally agreed only by myself. The financial haemorrhaging stopped immediately.

I called in the heavy lunchtime drinkers and said it was stop or out. They reformed at once and said they felt better with some leadership in the office.

Things improved generally, morale lifted and customer volumes climbed 10 per cent in six months. By tightening up stockholdings at the company-owned or leased service stations, a large sum of dead money was released into the bank account.

I instituted monthly performance and profit/loss figures for the company and introduced analyses of transport costs. At least we knew where we were going, although the destination and the length of the journey was indeterminate.

During this early period we pulled in more under-used money and had a particular success with a major oil supplier. They had been shipping our products by barge into our storage on the Thames and the problem involved the temperatures shown on loading certificates which seemed to me to be suspect. There should have been someone in the company watching loading data shown on those certificates. It is important to remember that the high temperature of a volume of gasoline means an inflated gallonage. Our cargoes were being received at a falsely high temperature. I was convinced that they were wrong and investigations by the dispatching company found that readings were being taken from the wrong temperature gauge. Thousands of pounds of value were involved. We welcomed the refunds.

Gasoline stock-keeping is a job for the esoteric and involves critical watch-keeping or one loses money. Heaven knows how much money had been lost in earlier years. How my father would have loved to get into such figure work!

The Chairman had a powerful presence and a good turn of phrase. He lived in a style in keeping with his love for old and new motor cars. He had been generous and effective in local affairs and sponsorships; however, his penchant for public relations activity and 'hand-outs' in a small company, as a stimulation for a modest turnover, did not coincide with my policy. Our Public Relations costs were out of synchronisation with revenue, profits and our share of the market.

I was not surprised to hear of outside interest in the company by the United Kingdom investment arm of a foreign oil group. I was party to some preliminary talks and thereafter we were examined in detail by the prospective buyer's team.

The leader of the new team reminded me of Roy Jenkins' description of Denis Healey in his biography *Life at the Centre*, as a large gun-carriage bearing a small cargo! One had to be patient but it was tiring. We managed finally to agree the state of the company and a deal was concluded by our Chairman in due course.

I continued as Managing Director for just three or four months. Clearly I was not the flavour of the month with the team leader nor was I deferential or quiescent enough for his directors.

I was still a member of the Council (a director in law) of the Institute of Petroleum (IP) and one evening in February 1984 I invited the new leader of the company management team to be my guest at the reception which preceded the Annual Dinner of the IP at the Grosvenor Hotel. On this occasion Mrs Thatcher, the Prime Minister, was the Guest of Honour. It was a very significant and prestigious occasion in international oil industry affairs, for it is an event which usually attracts 1,800 delegates, members and guests. We attended the reception for the Prime Minister but, as we were not dining, my 'friend' invited me to join him in the Grosvenor's La Fontaine Restaurant close by.

With exquisite timing during the dinner he told me I was fired and that my position as MD was nominal only and ephemeral. Unfortunately he had not consulted the minutes of a Board meeting, wherein it was stated that I was appointed to the post.

After some unpleasant exchanges over the next two weeks, compensation for loss of office was agreed, but the story does not quite end there. During the 'firing dinner' I was told that my successor had been appointed and it was believed that a good operator had been chosen.

As soon as he, the new MD, was installed in his office he began to drink a case of wine which his new principal had in store in the Managing Director's lavatory – for his own personal consumption. The new appointee polished it off before the owner could say: 'Hey! That's mine!'

Shortly afterwards the new incumbent was caught driving home whilst under the influence of alcohol. He continued driving after he was convicted at court and a while later was fired. I would have thought that the new leader's reputation might have suffered a bit of a dent!

My assisted departure was undeniably a botched job and my assignment came to its close in April 1986.

Michael Kemp, the motoring correspondent of the *Daily Mail*, reported to his readers that the company had changed hands 'for an eleven figure settlement'. Some settlement and some wildly inaccurate reporting!

For the next twenty months my time was taken up with a series of short assignments with small distributor companies based mainly in Southern England. But opportunities arose with ICI both in London and Billingham, as an expert witness, as a lecturer at Loughborough University and as an interviewee for the BBC.

I gave advice to a Bristol company who, luckily, introduced me to a consortium called Flare Petroleum which had a membership of fourteen companies. I was offered the post of Chief Executive and visited them all from time to time during my term of office. They were an interesting, hospitable, courageous and hardworking group of independent companies with whom I was fortunate to be associated. We held a dozen co-ordinating sales meetings in Solihull and one national sales conference in Worcester. I enjoyed the period of twenty months and withdrew when it appeared that I could do no more than they themselves already had in prospect

Within a few days of my resignation from Flare I had a call from my former chairman and I gave him lunch at the Royal Air Force Club; he was now, additionally, in the oil broking business and was of the opinion that his name and mine together had a useful aggregate of mileage in petroleum products distribution: a venture back into the trade we knew had particular potential and attraction. We came to terms.

I returned home with the news that I would start the new assignment on 1 September 1988, in London. The task involved the usual assembly of sales forecasts and their translation into profit/loss estimates. Thereafter the company was launched and began successfully to penetrate the market in Southern England.

It is always a thrill to be in at the beginning and this effort was no exception.

To give initial impetus to the surge forward, I was instructed to seek out and purchase a subsidiary company to give further strength to our growth in terms of tonnage and territory covered. A long-established private business was secured. With the new group well into the market-place in its chosen theatre of operation, I volunteered to undertake a further assignment with the same group in Canada in the city of Toronto. In this regard the shareholders were generous in taking my near-blind condition into account by agreeing that Mary should go with me.

I recommended a course of action for the Toronto business, which I believed to be in the group's short and medium term interest, and we returned home. The chairman successfully sold the distributor group some four or five years later.

During our stay in Toronto we were able to spend some time in the Maritime Provinces and flew to Halifax, Nova Scotia and St John, New Brunswick. Whilst in Halifax I called my POW friend, Kingsley Brown, then eighty-five years old, who failed to remember me! I also tried to trace the then young Canadian who had attempted suicide on a parole walk at Stalag Luft 3 in 1944, but failed to find him.

During our trip to St John, Mary and I took a boat to Partridge Island, just offshore. It was the equivalent in purpose in Canada (but not in size) as Ellis Island was to the US in New York harbour. Hopeful immigrants were landed and examined and those found to be unfit for admission were refused entry. There were many who had become so ill from the long voyage that they were hospitalised in an island building where they died. There have been burial services held to inter bones that have come to the surface of the ground. A very sad place where long held hopes were dashed for so many.

Back home business activities did not quite end. The following year, when I was seventy years old, I went to Romania for seven days; the purpose of this visit was to make a short review of the petroleum storage and distribution facilities in the most highly populated areas of that depressed country. My blindness was almost total, but I was provided with an interpreter and an escort. It was a revealing experience and in several ways it reminded me of Occupied Europe in 1943 – all the more disturbing in peacetime, forty-nine years later. Ceausescu was not long dead and no financial assistance had yet reached the country owing to the Presidency still being held by a one-time member of the previous Communist Government. Nothing was going to be done to help them until the Communist yoke was totally thrown off.

I found the Romanians with whom I worked to be kindly but greatly worried about their future, if and when Western help were to come. After forty years of Communist oppression and misrule they were resigned and baffled in a new situation which was taking them nowhere. When they heard first-hand from me of the rates of pay and conditions in the oil industry in the UK and the quality of life in general in the Western world, most of them shrugged and quietly showed resigned acceptance: it was useless to voice their feelings. They had thrown off the compulsory yoke of Communism but, as yet, there had been no lifting of the greyness of life and no steps forward on any front and I felt compassion for them.

All equipment was at least forty years old. There was no money to buy spare parts – even if they still existed – and new equipment was obviously impossible. Every failed part of oil industry plant and machinery had to be re-made from scratch with the materials available. The Ploesti oilfields were producing only a very moderate amount of crude; they are capable of further exploitation, but the new equipment needed was totally out of reach.

My Romanian friends insisted that I be shown round the pump-room in the oil installation at Busau. The chief engineer guided me round and I gained an impression of old but well maintained machinery. Yard surfaces were pitted and equipment everywhere must have been, from the descriptions given by my guide, decades past its 'sell by date'.

I visited a butane bottle-filling plant which would have been condemned immediately as dangerous and unfit in industrial terms in the western world. There was no ventilation in the roof of the building nor any air conditioning plant to deal with the heavily contaminated atmosphere. The only measure which recognised the foul working conditions was that all filling staff were given a special daily ration of fresh milk. Production of filled gas bottles was pitifully below national requirement and just the week before a Romanian had been killed outside the main gate in the fight to be first in line with his empty gas bottle.

At that time any recommendation that I made depended on the national ability to establish a viable economy. What is the use of replacing all the beaten up road tankers with new ones when only the showpiece roads are in reasonable shape and passable?

Why rebuild bottled-gas filling facilities when the oilfields could not increase production of petroleum gas? I do hope, several years later, that life is less hard for the friends who helped me.

I have memories of Romania still: in particular, they are about my entry and exit from that country. On arrival we awaited our luggage from the aircraft, but when it came, my bag could not be found. After a long search it was found by one of my party close to an enormous pile of dust-covered unclaimed cases in a dark corner of the baggage area. We all had the impression that this positioning was deliberate and had the case not been found, it would have been looted before being thrown on the pile.

Thereafter, we joined a long queue to be admitted to Romania and had to pay $40 for an entry and exit permit. When we left the country, armed soldiers within the half-lit terminal all wanted to carry our bags for a dollar. I felt very relieved that I had not lost my exit permit!

In those times the number of electric light bulbs that could be used in any home or establishment was set out under the law. As a result I found it impossible to reach my hotel room without help, which was willingly given.

One day I was halfway through my morning ablutions when the water was turned off (a regular happening at 7 am). I was caught on that occasion, but I managed to finish shaving with the aid of a bottle of aerated water!

During my stay at an hotel in another location, I discovered that the bottom sheet of my bed covered only half the length of the mattress. My feet had been lying on the mattress at the bottom of the bed where generations of other feet had rested!

I hope more lights are now on in Romania and some good steps forward have been made to give the people of that country a better life. The human spirit always wins, but so often at such a price. I believe I know something about that particular issue.

In September 1992 I received a note from the Institute of Directors, of which I was then a member, asking me if I would join a team at the Henley Management College and take part in the study of Standards for UK Boards of Directors. The Department of Education had asked the Institute of Directors to pursue this study and to produce a code of practice. The College was briefed to produce such a code for the Institute and the document entitled *Good Practice for Boards of Directors* was published in early 1994.

My loss of sight proved to be no inhibition and my short venture into academia as a self-taught individual was enlightening and the opportunity to make a contribution brought me quiet satisfaction. I am still ingenuous enough to feel that my part in this minor, but worthy, task brought my working life to an end on a note of respectability. This, I hope was further sealed by my being invited to submit a career summary for an entry in Debrett's *People of Today*.

Epilogue

We survivors and flying colleagues came together in the early autumn of 1942 and remain friends in fact and spirit to this day. It is a far cry from those days when we were emptied into a large pool of men, each charged with the same duty of finding six other potential friends to make up the crew of a fighting aircraft. Each one of us found six colleagues whom we came to like and then to respect, to trust and value both for their proficiency and for their friendship.

As it happened, when the conflict was over, we were to have concern for each other as we aged. But our contentment and relief at being survivors is tempered by the deaths of two of our comrades. Ronnie Chisholm, our American tail-gunner to whom, in all probability, we owe our lives, died in Seattle in tragic circumstances in 1945, shortly after he returned home; Duggie Inggs, our radio operator, died in 1992, the victim of a very trying illness. Very fortunately, but very late in the day, we had a re-union of the six survivors in 1988 at the Royal Air Force Club in Piccadilly. Cecil Anderson came over from Canada for the event and, save for his wife Betty, there were five wives present: Mary, Dorothy Evans, Peggy Taylor, Marjorie Henderson and Margaret Inggs. The whole episode was very special and not without its emotional moments.

Our daughter Catherine took me to Gatwick to meet Cecil flying in from Edmonton, Alberta. When he arrived at the airport he said: 'After forty-five years all I knew was that I had to look for a tall guy!'

There is no doubt that each one of us has made a mark in his lifetime and has a story to tell. I would have had no book in me, nor the honour of having a place in their memories, had we not come together in that haphazard – or officially inspired – way at Royal Air Force Upper Heyford. The memory of our time as a crew has been the distant backdrop to each of our lives, whatever the current event thereafter.

The main events of my own life are set out in this narrative but there is a little more to say as it has been my aim to try fairly to reveal my own traits and idiosyncrasies.

In 1952 the War Pensions Authority referred the matter of the onset of my blindness and their prognosis to St Dunstans, the charity set up in 1915 to care for ex-servicemen and women whose sight had been lost or was severely damaged. For some time thereafter I was invited to report annually both to the St Dunstans and to the War Pensions' ophthalmic specialists. In the latter case the authorities were very fair and, as my condition worsened, my disability pension increased.

St Dunstans invitations petered out after a few years and were not resumed until 1977 when, it was said, my file had been found gathering dust in the cellars of their headquarters building. As a result of this visit, when my eyes were re-examined, I was admitted as a beneficiary of the charity on 28 February 1977, three-plus years after the loss of my company, Trident Petroleum and during my toughest struggles to gain a living and a career footing in consultancy in the oil industry.

Gentle pressure was applied to me by the charity to go to their training centre at Ovingdean near Brighton. I resisted this for a while but was eventually persuaded to visit there for talks.

At this first meeting I agreed to go for training for a period of three months. As a near blind person it was one of the best decisions I ever made. I was told I would be trained to touch type and taught Braille; I could not then appreciate how typing would have any profound effect on my need to face the remainder of my life as a blind man. However, I succeeded in the execution of a typing test and the first stage ability test in Braille. My pleasure at these achievements was entirely out of synchronisation with my reluctance to start any training.

Almost at the end of my stay at St Dunstans I had lessons in personal mobility when outdoors. The final test for this was the total avoidance of a ducking in a pond in a public garden used by St Dunstans as a training ground in nearby Brighton. I escaped a wetting and went home to the Manor House and began to write better quality typewritten letters.

It is perfectly true that the training I had at Ovingdean taught me to accept the fact of loss of sight and set me on the path of overcoming blindness. I did not, at first, like carrying a white stick – known as the symbol cane. I felt awkward about it and was reluctant to use it. However, an incident at Waterloo Station cured me of that problem. One day when I descended from a train there, the heavy elastic cord which holds the stick together and which enables it to be folded up, broke as I stepped down to the platform and attempted to unfold it. The four parts of the stick fell with a ringing sound in all directions. Each one of four kind individuals picked up one piece – my inhibitions were over!

One embarrassing incident is also worth reporting: I finished lunch one day in the main dining-room of the Royal Air Force Club and had begun to leave. As I passed a large dessert trolley near the exit I was offered help by one of the staff. Momentarily caught off-balance I instinctively put out my left hand to find a steadying object of some kind. My hand went deeply into a bowl of standard sherry trifle!

'I am so sorry.'

'Never mind, Sir. Let me wipe your hand.'

As the record in this book shows, I survived the period from the loss of Trident in 1973 to retirement in 1991 and during that time the pace of life did not slacken overall. Throughout the longer periods of assignment to client companies, I was fortunate to have a car and driver provided. During the last appointment my chauffeuse came from the Women's Royal Army Corps – and how very good she was!

In forty years of passenger travel in motor cars I have, from time to time, quietly mourned the loss of freedom one suffers when one cannot walk out to a car and drive away. There is another side to that coin however: I feel deep down that I am a lazy person and that my disability has been a spur to make me go forward.

But how is life affected now? I cannot read or write, except with the help of my trusty word processor and friendly voice synthesizer; toothpaste is squeezed into the palm of the hand and scooped up with the head of the toothbrush, selected from two by the shape of the plastic grip; suits are selected by feeling for the texture and weight of cloth (not entirely reliable); cuff buttons, turn-ups on trousers (or not) and small identifying items in breast-pockets help with identification. In summer short sleeve shirts are hung first in line on the rail and one can detect coloured items by slightly heavier material. Ordinary shirts to go with a certain suit are difficult to find but there is one sure-fire method: 'Help!'

Brown shoe-polish is at the back of a box and black to the front. A straight line to one's sideburns can be kept by shaving up to the underside of the cheekbone just forward of the ear and no further!

Most importantly, food is positioned on the plate at the four quarter point positions and a wine glass can only have one position at 2 o'clock to the plate – too many glasses have been up-ended and broken. A large white napkin is mandatory at all times; nothing is moved from its usual position without due notice. A little progress is made each day – save for the local disasters!

St Dunstaners and other blind non-service people who have no hearing, no hands and have lost limbs, keep one's own difficulties in perspective. A good St Dunstaner friend who lost his sight, his hearing and his right arm and has only three fingers on his left hand – injuries sustained in Northern Ireland – said to me recently that he would rather have lost his sight as he did and did not envy my two-stage battle of gradual loss and the second more telling one of complete blackout. Every situation in life has its own yardsticks of comparison!

The single most helpful instrument in my blindness is my computer word-processor and the voice synthesizer. It is a friend which demands perfect performance and unhesitatingly indicates when one attempts to put rubbish into print. It is the right tool for me, for I am seldom totally satisfied with my work.

Courage and bravery can be found amongst the younger generation of today where one finds a visually impaired unit in a school. The children display such high levels of determination, often against shatteringly difficult family backgrounds and harassment at school. The levels of competence and confidence present in the younger generations today is repeated in equal measure amongst blind children. I have presented prizes to such children and have watched them growing in stature and ability throughout their schooling. Blindness is put in its place by all generations.

The children must have the last say. I have given many talks to school groups taking European History in GCSE. They are excellent audiences. One hopes that they will remember the hardship undergone by the occupied countries. Their questions have been realistic but two gems from young pupils are appropriate here:

'How did you feel on the day war broke out?'

'Full of foreboding.'

'Did you ever meet Hitler?'

'No, I did not – thankfully.'